BY THE SAME AUTHOR

General
The Savage God: A Study of Suicide
Under Pressure: The Writer in Society: Eastern Europe and the USA
Life After Marriage: Scenes from Divorce
The Biggest Game in Town
Offshore: A North Sea Journey
Rain Forest (with paintings by Charles Blackman)
Night: An Exploration of Night Life, Night Language,
Sleep and Dreams
Poker: Bets, Bluffs and Bad Beats

Novels
Hers
Hunt
Day of Atonement

Poetry
Lost
Penguin Modern Poets, No. 18
Apparition (with paintings by Charles Blackman)
Autumn to Autumn and Selected Poems 1953–76
New and Selected Poems

Criticism
The Shaping Spirit (*US title*: Stewards of Excellence)
The School of Donne
Beyond All This Fiddle: Essays 1955–1967
Samuel Beckett

Anthologies (*editor*)
The New Poetry
The Faber Book of Modern European Poetry

Autobiography
Where Did It All Go Right?

FEEDING THE RAT
PROFILE OF A CLIMBER

AL ALVAREZ

BLOOMSBURY

First published in Great Britain 1988
This paperback edition published 2003

Parts of this book originally appeared in
slightly different form in the NewYorker

Picture credits
The author and publishers are grateful to the following for permission to
reproduce photographs: Mo Anthoine, nos 2, 4, 5, 6, 7; John Cleare/
Mountain Camera, nos 1, 10; Hamish MacInnes, nos 3, 8, 9; Chris
Mikami/ CM Photography, nos 11, 12.

Grateful acknowledgement is made to Bloodaxe Books for permission
to reprint 'Love' by Miroslav Holub, translated by Ian Milner, from
Miroslav Holub, *Poems Before and After: Collected English Translations*
(Bloodaxe Books, 1990)

'The 'Old Man' and The Voice' by Jane Kramer first published by
Los Poetry Press, Great Britain 1999

Epilogue by Al Alvarez first published by Thunder's Mouth Press,
New York 2001

Bloomsbury Publishing plc, 38 Soho Square, London W1D 3HB

A CIP catalogue is available from the British Library

ISBN 0 7475 6452 3

10 9 8 7 6 5 4 3 2 1

Printed in Great Britain by Clays Ltd, St Ives, plc

CONTENTS

ILLUSTRATIONS

INTRODUCTION

The 'Old Man' and the Voice

Long before I knew Al, I had an Al Alvarez epiphany. I was flying to Europe on one of those cheap Air Icelandic student flights – call it the last propeller – that took twenty-two hours and stopped in Reykjavik to refuel. It was no place for a book. No one over twenty-five ever flew Air Icelandic. No one who did sat down. You danced in the aisle, drank, smoked, groped and fell in love. Reading on a twenty-two hour flight to Europe was the airborne equivalent of Saturday night alone, at home, by the telephone.

But not this time. Maybe it was the recession, maybe the season, but the only children on the flight were babies. I spent fourteen or fifteen hours staring into the sky, and then we landed in Reykjavik's tiny airport. Icelanders, having no diversions besides other Icelanders, are famous for reading books, so I went into the terminal to find one. I can't remember the book I actually bought – I think it was Bunyan, but it doesn't matter, and in the event it isn't the Bunyan I have now. (Bookcases are a sign of age; your old books begin to look as old as you do, a little worn, a little flaking and faded, and you find yourself thinking, 'Wait a minute! I only bought that thirty years ago', and then you replace it and look younger).

What I do remember is the shock of reading the

introduction. It was an absolutely ravishing piece of prose. It made a short novel out of the bones of a barely-known life, an adventure out of an exegesis. It was so seamless that it even looked seamless. When I searched for some dates – even some centuries would have helped – I couldn't find them, and this, as they say, was something I could relate to. Whoever wrote that introduction hadn't wanted to see any ugly numbers sticking up in the middle of his sentences. When I got to a name, way over on the right at the bottom of page xxxiv, give or take a Roman numeral, I met Al Alvarez. He became my mentor. I wish he had been on the plane.

Now that we're friends, it's Al who seems seamless. Reading him is like a long visit without the poker, unless, of course, you're reading about the poker. Al has what the kids call attitude and the rest of us call voice – as in 'Henry James had a voice'. He is, of course, a novelist and a poet and an essayist and a critic, and he knows all about voice. But as a reporter I know how difficult it is to carve out and carry a voice in what the universities call the 'literature of fact' – i.e., long journalism – unless it's the voice of some dreadful confessional or the voice of an ego invading its own story. There isn't one word of a piece of Al Alvarez's non-fiction that loses its voice or makes you say, 'Wait a minute, Al, move over.' On the other hand, there isn't a word that doesn't sound like Al talking.

Sometimes, when I'm teaching, I start the course with Al's first paragraph in *Feeding the Rat* the one that begins: 'Llanberis is a small, dank town squeezed between the uninviting waters of Llyn Padarn and the grassy lower slopes of Snowdon, the highest mountain in Wales.' That, to me, is the journalistic equivalent of 'Call Me Ishmael' or 'Happy families are all alike; every unhappy family is unhappy in it's own way.' It's descriptive. It's direct. It's true. It doesn't stoop to the passive or, God forbid, cheat the way I do with adverbs. There are a couple of adjectives, but they're not fancy; they're clean adjectives, and they're clues. They set the theme. 'Small' takes you right to the second paragraph: one main street and a couple of fish-and chipperies. 'Dank' that's paragraph three, where it always rains. So is 'uninviting': Llanberis's lake is dammed up and lit by a glare from nightlights in a tunnel to a hydroelectric plant. 'Grassy' and 'lower' mean that our hero, Mo Anthoine, and his wife, Jackie – paragraph four – will have some relief from their eyesore of a town, and 'highest', of course, means that Mo wouldn't live anywhere else. Mo is a rock climber, like Al. The rat is his addiction to hanging off rocks. This is a book about climbing.

The students don't know this, but the voice in *Feeding the Rat* is the one that Al's friends put up with because it feeds his prose. You could call it 'the voice of the old man'. Been there, done that, paid my dues. Al was no more than forty-five when we really did meet, but he was already referring to himself as 'the old man'. I imagine he was doing it back in the days I was flying Air Icelandic. 'The old man' is by definition a man's voice, with its high regard for the foolhardy and possibly the fatal. But I don't know any man except Al who carries it off without a trace of the cracker, the Hemingway, or that awful bravura that makes all women roll their eyes. Al's 'old man' doesn't posture. He's too smart. He's already asked the hard, deep questions, settled his score with questions, and dismissed them. It's a voice that knows.

Al, of course, never talks about voice. That's what makes him an agreeable friend and a writer whose sentences make you gasp at how much they hold. I wouldn't want to climb a pebble, but *Feeding the Rat* makes me feel not so much that it's worth it but that there are people who do, and for them it's worth it. I wouldn't want to be the patsy in one of Al's poker games, either. (I saw that coming a couple of years ago in Italy, when Al called saying that, oddly enough, 'the guys' were in Italy, too, and my house 'seemed to be equidistant'). But *The Biggest Game in Town* and Al's poker pieces for *The New Yorker* are the closest anyone's gotten to that particular rat. They teach you the character of the game and, more important, the character of the outrageous people who play it. They are object-lessons in the meaningless dignity of risk.

There is another side to the Alvarez voice. It's about praxis. Cowboys call this quality 'expressing right'. Al has it, and the people he admires and turns to prose usually have it, too. Mo Anthoine. A couple of mad tournament gamblers. His neighbour Alfred Brendel. (One of Al's best *New Yorker* pieces is his portrait of Brendel, practising the piano). They are all people who have managed to locate in themselves the source of some elegant economy of gesture and person, a way of being who they are, how they reason, what they do, and how they do it. You could say that, like Al's writing, they've shed the excess, that nothing about their work, or their judgement, or their art is extraneous.

Think Bill Clinton; then think Jimmy Stewart and you'll see what the cowboys mean. Think *Feeding the Rat* and you'll see what I mean. That mountain of details about climbing a mountain – details that would ground you in anyone else's hands – takes you climbing. It's Al expressing right. Nothing is wasted. The height of a spire. The name of a rope. The colour of a certain sandstone. All the exotic words of an exotic sport turning into language. You have to listen to every one, and you miss them when you get back down to the grassy foothills. I tried to count the number of times 'old man' – or, for that matter, 'young hotshot' – appears in *Feeding the Rat*, but I gave up early, because Al is sly. His old man covers for the hotshot. You have to watch him.

Jane Kramer, 1999

1
Llanberis

L lanberis is a small, dank town squeezed between the uninviting waters of Llyn Padarn and the grassy lower slopes of Snowdon, the highest mountain in Wales. At the eastern end of town, opposite the stately Royal Victoria Hotel, is a railway station and from it, in summer, small trains loaded with tourists chug slowly to the top of Snowdon where there is a gloomy café and a marvellous view. Snowdon and its railway account for the fact that Llanberis has half a dozen hotels and at least twice that many guest houses, as well as souvenir shops, a shop that sells Welsh crafts – mostly wool and sheepskin – and an elegant restaurant called Y Bistro which has an ambitious chef and a menu in two languages, English and Welsh.

But there is not much else about the place to attract tourists, least of all the weather, which is generally dreadful. On the winding main street the dingy, gabled terraced houses outnumber the dingy, gabled terraced shops, and the pubs are bleak and stripped for action. There are two fish-and-chipperies, one Chinese take-away, and Pete's Eats, a café with permanently steamed-up windows where they serve good bacon sandwiches and pint mugs of strong tea.

The houses of Llanberis have one thing in common, apart from the mournful, tear-stained look that comes from month after month of rain: by municipal ordinance, all of them are neatly roofed with slate tiles. These days the tiles are mostly brought in from elsewhere, but for years the main source of work for the locals was in the vast slate quarries that terrace the hills on the other side of Llyn Padarn. But the quarries closed in 1969, the lake was dammed, and a hydroelectric plant was built deep beneath the hills from which the slate was once hacked. The tunnel that leads down to the generators is brightly lit at night and when you drive into town it shines ominously across the lake, as in the establishing shots of a nuclear disaster movie. When the quarries closed Llanberis became a depressed area with an unemployment rate exceptional even for Wales. In summer the biggest employer is now the Snowdon railway; for the rest of the year, the main source of work in Llanberis is a company called Snowdon Mouldings, which currently has a staff of twenty-three.

Snowdon Mouldings is owned by Mo Anthoine and his wife Jackie, and it has been growing steadily since 1968 when Mo and Joe Brown, the greatest of all British climbers, began making Joe Brown safety helmets in the cellar of Brown's house in Llanberis. The company gradually spread into a nearby cottage, then subdivided into a converted chapel in the Scottish Highlands when Mo diversified into ice-axes, and is now back in Llanberis in another converted chapel, this one much larger in order to cope with a range of products which has expanded to include tents and all sorts of outdoor clothing.

Apart from Y Bistro and its nearness to Snowdon, Llanberis has one other tourist attraction: Joe Brown's shop. It is not large but, with its slate floors and stripped-pine fittings, it seems disproportionately fancy for its situation. So do its contents: racks of down jackets, shelves piled with sleeping bags and expensive sweaters, a room lined with boxes of mountain boots, brightly coloured ropes hanging in coils from the ceiling, a wall festooned with carabiners, nuts, pitons, slings and chalk bags, shelves of climbing guides and assorted mountaineering literature. It is a kind of Aladdin's cave for mountaineers, and most weekends, particularly when the weather is bad, the place is packed with young hopefuls covetously fingering the goods and gossiping in the close-mouthed, bristly way that is peculiar to the climbing world.

Although Llanberis is no longer the main source of slate for the British Isles, it is still the centre for British climbing. Over the years, the native Welsh population has been steadily supplemented by a flow of young Englishmen – the majority of them from the north and all of them self-made internal exiles, like Russian dissidents – who have gone there to climb and then stayed on, taking odd jobs to keep themselves fed. Because climbers as a group tend to be highly motivated, competent and independent (they would not otherwise survive in the hills), they are usually good at whatever work they take up. As a result, the plumbing, carpentry, bricklaying, roofing and decorating are probably better, and certainly cheaper, in Llanberis than anywhere else in Britain. There is only one problem: climbing comes before money, so in good weather work gets delayed.

Since 1966, Mo Anthoine has lived in the village of Nant Peris–a church, a pub, a general store and a scattering of houses–a couple of miles east of Llanberis. He is now forty-eight years old and his untidy mop of hair is greying at the edges. He is short–five feet seven inches–and slightly top-heavy in build: deep chest, arms like logs, surprisingly spindly legs. His shoulder muscles –the deltoids and *latissimi dorsi*–are so highly developed that when he stretches out his arms he looks as if he were about to take off. He has a seventeen-inch neck and never wears a tie because he is convinced that no shirt that fits his neck will fit him anywhere else. His head is big and square and intelligent, his chin is small, and his upper lip seems to be equipped with an extra set of muscles that enable it to twist and curl like a Hallowe'en mask –apparently, all by itself. He has blue eyes but there is a fleck of brown in the left eye that looks disconcertingly like a spot of blood. Years ago, he had back trouble so severe that he finally, and with great misgiving, booked himself into hospital for surgery on his spine; luckily for him, the discs fused together a few days before the operation and the pain disappeared; but since that time he has walked like a sailor, with a rolling, sway-backed gait and no movement at all in the lower spine. He wears jeans, T-shirt and trainers, whatever the weather, and owns only one suit which he shares with his friend, Joe

Brown. This means that they can never go to the same
funeral or wedding. It is an arrangement that pleases
them both.

Mo was christened Julian and acquired his nickname
when he was four years old. He got it from one of the
Three Stooges – 'the nasty one with the fringe,' he says
– and it stuck. He also says, 'With a name like Julian
you'd want it to stick, wouldn't you?' He was born
in Kidderminster in 1939 and, in a way, he has been
going on expeditions since he was eleven years old. His
mother died when he was four and his stepmother was
a Dickensian tyrant. 'By the time I was ten I was doing
all the dusting and Hoovering and ironing,' he says. 'I
was cleaning the grate, polishing the shoes, peeling the
potatoes. So anything that got me out of the house I
leapt at. I joined the Boy Scouts and they took me
camping. That was a real breakthrough: it meant that
I could get away from home and also enjoy myself. For
a few bob I bought myself an ex-US Army bivouac
tent and I used to go away every weekend. I'd pack a
rucksack, go off on my own on Saturday morning, and
not come back until Sunday night. In those days, a ten-
minute walk would get you out of Kidderminster and
into the wilds. I used to camp at the edge of the River
Severn – places like that. And for some reason, Win,
my stepmother, never minded. Nowadays, of course,
you'd never let a kid of eleven go off on his own, but
thirty-five years ago it didn't seem to be a problem.'

Like many children who are kept under at home,
Mo was wild at school, and he dropped out just

before he sat the exams that would have qualified him for university. His father was a tiny, clever man, an amateur painter who chain-smoked and had a passion for music and chess. He designed carpets for a living, and Mo, after a few months with a civil engineering firm in Birmingham, joined him as a trainee manager in the carpet industry. He was seventeen years old. Two years later, he discovered climbing.

'As part of the management training, they sent you on an Outward Bound course,' he says. 'It was the daftest thing they ever did with me.' For some people, climbing can be an addiction that alters the psyche's chemistry as surely as heroin alters the body's. At the end of a month at Outward Bound school in Aberdovey, Mo was hooked. He began to climb every weekend, hitching up to Wales after work on Friday evening, returning Sunday night. Gradually, the week-ends began to get longer, starting Thursday evening, ending Monday night. His employers did not complain, and perhaps did not even notice but, even so, when his summer holiday came round and he went off for the first time to the Alps, that was the end of his career in carpets.

He had also decided that he had had enough of Win and it was time to leave home. He left a message on the kitchen table to say he wasn't coming back, and when the friends he had gone to the Alps with returned to England he set off, with £12 in his pocket, to hitch-hike to New Zealand, 'to see what the ice climbing was like'. From an atlas in the Kidderminster library, he had compiled a list of the towns on the west coast of Africa, 'so I'd know where to hitch to,' he explains. 'I thought that if I could reach Cape Town I could find a job, because they were English-speaking, and from there I'd get myself across to Australia and New Zealand.'

As it turned out, he got no farther than Casablanca, where everything he had was stolen, except for his passport. The surly British consul refused to help him, so he hitched, starving, back to England.

He spent the rest of the summer climbing in North Wales, then volunteered for the Marines. (He says, 'They gave me an IQ test a chimp could have passed, and told me I should go for a commission.') But by the time his orders came to report for basic training, he was enjoying himself too much in the hills. He phoned the Marine barracks from a call-box in Nant Peris and said he wasn't coming.

'You've signed the papers,' they said. 'They're legally binding.'

'Tough.'

'Where are you?'

'That's for me to know and you to find out,' he said and hung up.

He took a job as an instructor at Ogwen Cottage, a climbing school below Tryfan, a mountain not far from Snowdon. The pay was 10 shillings a week, plus his keep and all the climbing he could manage, and he took it on a strictly temporary basis. 'I told myself that as soon as I got to regard instructing as being just a job, I'd pack it in,' he says. 'I didn't want to lose my feeling for climbing–I didn't want it ruined.'

Two years later, in 1961, he decided that he was, indeed, bored and again set off to hitch-hike to New Zealand, this time with £35 in his pocket and a climbing rope in his rucksack. He went with a friend, Ian Cartledge–otherwise known as Fox because he had reddish hair–and the journey there and back took them two years. They hitched across Europe, Turkey and Iran, into Baluchistan, Pakistan and India, up to Nepal, down into Burma, on to Malaya and Thailand, across to Australia, and, finally, on to the South Island of New Zealand for the ice climbing. They lived dirt cheap (in India they budgeted on 1 shilling a day), refused on principle to pay for any transport except ships, and took jobs where they could find them: an Iranian paid them to smuggle turquoise into Pakistan; they spent four months digging culverts for a new railway in northern Queensland; they worked in a blue asbestos mine in Wittenoom Gorge in Western Australia. (Of that potentially lethal experience Mo now says philosophically, 'It's a long incubation period, thank God. About twenty-six years. So I've still got a year or two to go!') To get back home they crewed on a yacht across the Indian Ocean, jumped ship in Aden, crossed to Djibouti, hitch-hiked up through East Africa into Egypt, then on through Cyprus into Greece. The last stage of the journey, from Athens to Ripley, in Derbyshire, took them a mere three

and a half days–which was just as well since it was
an unusually cold spring and by then Mo's wardrobe
was reduced to a shirt, shorts, and a pair of leopard-
skin slippers he had had made in Khartoum for 10
shillings.

2
The Dolomites

Back in England, Mo decided to train as a teacher – teaching being an occupation that would guarantee him plenty of time off for climbing. He spent a probationary period, teaching P.E. and Maths, to see if he liked the work, then three years, beginning in the autumn of 1964, at Coventry College of Education. I first met him in August of that year, in the Dolomites, at a run-down little hut directly below the south faces of the Tre Cime di Lavoredo. We had arrived there independently with partners who both decided, after one short route, that they preferred to lie in the sun outside the hut and leave the climbing to others. Mo was ten years younger than me, and a much better climber, so I grabbed the chance to be led up some hard routes. As for Mo, he didn't seem to mind which routes he did as long as he climbed.

Rock climbing is one of the purest, least cluttered of sports, and requires a minimum of equipment: a pair of special boots, a rope, a safety helmet, and a collection of nylon slings and metal gear – carabiners (snap links), pitons, étriers (stirrups) and alloy nuts – with which you try to protect yourself in case of a fall. The whole lot costs relatively little, lasts for years and hangs easily around your neck and from your waist. So climbing is unlike many sports in that if anything goes wrong the fault is usually in you, not in your gear. But then climbing, according to Mo, isn't a sport at all. 'It's a pastime,' he says. 'It involves pleasure. Whereas a sport, by definition, involves competition. In climbing, the only competition is with yourself'–that is, with your protesting muscles, your nerves and, when things go wrong, with your reserves of character. It is even, in its way, an intellectual activity, though with one important qualification: you have to think with your body. Each pitch is a series of specific local problems: which holds to use, and in which combinations, in order to get up safely and with the least expenditure of energy. Every move has to be worked out by a kind of physical strategy, in terms of effort, balance and consequences. It is like playing chess with your body.

A solitary pastime, then, but one that, for safety's sake, usually involves someone else. (Some of the top performers like to climb entirely on their own–they call it 'soloing'–but that is a high-risk activity I never aspired to, even in my dotty youth.) So whom you climb with matters almost as much as what you climb, particularly since who influences how. Some climbers are so driven by their desire to get up a route that they are indifferent to everything and everyone else; climbing with them is like being strapped to the outside of a monorail express–you reach your destination but there aren't a lot of laughs along the way and you don't see much of the landscape. Others are so unsure of their own abilities that their only pleasure seems to be when their partner has trouble on a move they themselves have found easy. Others are plain unsafe and are constantly pushing themselves beyond their natural limits or failing to take obvious precautions. Climbers who survive and go on climbing usually grow out of these weaknesses as they get older; but before they do so life on the rope with them can be nasty, brutish and short.

When Mo was in his twenties he had a reputation as a wild man – 'My mother died of cirrhosis of the liver and never drank a drop, so I did my best to redress the balance!' – but there was nothing wild about the way he climbed. Our first route was the Spigolo Giallo, one of the most beautiful of all Dolomite climbs, straight up the south-facing 'yellow edge' of the Anticima of the Cima Piccola di Lavoredo, about 1,000 feet long and plumb vertical most of the way. Mo did the leading and every so often he would pause and call down, 'That's an ace bit!' or, 'You're gonna love this!' That invariably meant that he had just done a hard move, but his progress was so steady that the difficulties, when I came to them, became part of the enjoyment and I found that I was climbing better than I usually did. The last pitch was easy and spectacular – on big holds up a vertical wall, with nothing but air and the wheeling swallows between my feet and the scree far below. When I pulled over the top Mo was propped against a boulder, enjoying the afternoon sun, his shirt off and a cigarette in his mouth. 'Happiness is a VS to heaven,' he said. (In those days, VS, Very Severe, was, in effect, the top grade but one in the British climbing classification, which went from

Moderate, through Difficult, Very Difficult, Severe, Very Severe, to Hard Very Severe, with just a handful of climbs classified as Extreme. Since then, standards have risen and Extreme is now subdivided numerically into as many grades as all the rest put together.) 'A VS to heaven' is as good a way as any of describing that sense of freedom and lightness, both mental and physical, that comes when everything is going as it should on rock that is hard but not too hard – when tension dissolves, movement seems effortless, every risk seems under control, and your own inner silence is like that of the mountains themselves.

A couple of days later, we went round to the other, more serious side of the Cima Grande to try the classic Comici route, up the North Face. It is nearly twice as long as the Spigolo Giallo, technically harder and considerably steeper. The first 800 feet of it lean steadily outwards – a stone dropped from the top of this overhanging section would hit the scree below thirty feet out from the base – and the upper part is like a huge open book of stone: a 1,000-foot vertical crack in a corner. The night before, Mo had been 'redressing the balance' – with my help – so we overslept, started late, were held up by two slow parties in front of us, and then were caught in a snowstorm when we were 600 feet up the overhangs and beyond any point of return. We spent the night belayed to a small ledge, a couple of feet long and eighteen inches wide, 500 feet from the top.

Because this was August in Italy and the previous route had gone easily, we were climbing light – that is, we were carrying neither food nor extra clothing. A waterfall of melting snow was cascading down the long final crack and, although the ledge we finished on was protected by an overhang, we were soaked to the skin by the time we stopped. We took off our shirts, wrung them out, put them back on, and settled down for a long night, while the gunmetal clouds lifted, the stars came out and the air froze. It was important not to sleep because sleep lowers the body's temperature, so we talked, sang songs, swapped limericks. Even so, we kept dozing off, then waking, disorientated, to continue the singsong, hearing our voices become frailer and more impertinent in the engulfing darkness. Some time around three o'clock, we woke again to find something had changed. The moon was down, the valley far below was a pool of ink, the distant peaks were blue-black against the starry sky. But it was not just the quality of the darkness that had altered; the silence, too, had deepened, become impenetrable. We huddled together, trying to work out what had happened.

Then Mo said, 'The waterfall's frozen.'

At that point, I concluded that our luck had run out and that we, too, would soon be frozen. I didn't say so at the time, of course, but when I mentioned it to Mo months later he was astonished. 'It was a bit parky,' he said, 'but it never occurred to me that we were in real trouble.' His attitude was: we're all right for the moment, so we'd better do what we can to stay that way. We pummelled each other to restore the circulation, blew on our hands, and smoked continuously

–both to allay our hunger and for the comfort of it. (It is amazing how warm tobacco feels when you are freezing.) Even so, the dawn was a long time coming: first a vague, pale shadow that might have been cloud at the edge of the rock wall that shut us in, then an infinitely slow seeping away of blackness into grey. The last 500 feet to the top seemed disproportionately hard. There were plaques of verglas in some of the places where there should have been holds and both of us were frost-bitten – Mo in the feet, me in the fingers.

It sounds dramatic – night on the bare mountain, a frozen waterfall, frostbite. In fact, it was nothing of the kind – largely because Mo seemed to assume that what was happening was perfectly normal. He was cheerful and casual, and he kept the one-liners coming. Egged on by him, I killed a half hour by reciting a complete version, with variants, of 'The Ballad of Eskimo Nell', and when I tried complaining about the smallness of the ledge we were tied to – each with one buttock on, one off – all Mo said was, 'Well, you can't have everything.' It was the coldest night I have ever sat through, and one of the most uncomfortable, but it was by no means the gloomiest.

Climbing is a strong example of what is called 'deep play'. The phrase is Jeremy Bentham's and he, as the father of utilitarianism, profoundly disapproved of the concept. In deep play the stakes are so high that, in Bentham's view, it is irrational for anyone to engage in it at all, since the marginal utility of what you stand to win is grossly outweighed by the disutility of what you stand to lose. In our case, the gain was the dubious satisfaction of having climbed a difficult route in difficult conditions; what we stood to lose was our toes, or our fingers, or even our lives.

Yet, however deep the play was, it was still play, and that is mostly how I remember it. I remember the laconic one-liners and the limericks, the comically small ledge festooned with gear, the moonlit distant peaks, the marvellous taste of pipe tobacco, and the little pools of warmth and light we created each time we lit a match. But my clearest memory of all is of a moment on the second morning, and it has nothing to do with freezing to death. In those days, nuts were not things you could buy in shops; you had to find them – junked cars were the best source – drill them out and thread them on to your own slings. Mo left one on the last pitch that was so deep in a crack that nothing I could do with my swollen, frost-bitten fingers would shift it.

'I can't get it out,' I shouted, and started on up the crack.

'Oh,' said Mo, and his voice was so small and depressed that I looked up. He was peering down at me and, for the first time since we had been on the mountain, the expression on his face was stricken.

'It's my favourite nut,' he said.

Well, I thought, it's my favourite life. I owe him one. So I went back down and spent twenty minutes prodding around with a piton hammer until the nut came free. Since he had done all the leading, it seemed the least I could do.

When we got to the summit we lay for a while in the sun and watched our wet clothes steam. I felt exhausted beyond exhaustion and slightly light-headed – surprised, I suppose, to be alive. As we set off to scramble down the easy south side of the mountain, Mo said, 'Right. We're halfway there.'

'Pardon?'

'This is when accidents happen,' he said. 'When you've got to the top and start relaxing.'

It was odd how completely our roles had reversed. I was the one in his middle thirties and he was supposed to be the wild man. But, clearly, in the mountains his wildness did not apply.

3
Epics

Maybe Mo acquired his respect for danger, along with his self-reliance, when he went off camping on his own as a child and realized that if he did not take care of himself no one else would. Whatever its source, it is not something he has learned the hard way, by hurting himself. In twenty-nine years of difficult routes, he has never once fallen off – in itself some kind of record in an activity that is second only to Formula One racing in its turnover of stars.

His ability to calculate the risks and act accordingly seems to have been in place from the start of his mountaineering career. Four years before our episode in the Dolomites, for example, he and a companion had set out to do a route on the Brenva Face of Mont Blanc. Like all big Alpine routes, it involved leaving the hut long before dawn and climbing the initial, easy terrain in the dark. But because this was his first Alpine season and he was, anyway, penniless, he and his partner had only the most elementary equipment. Instead of using head torches, they tried to light their way with an ancient, mica-paned candle lantern that blew out the moment they left the hut. 'We were very frightened by that and came straight back,' he says. 'I'm still glad I had the sense to back off it, although I was disappointed at the time.'

Safety, however, is not what the general public is after. In 1970, Mo went on his first major expedition, to El Toro in the Peruvian Andes. The climbers got to within one rope-length of the top and all that was left was an easy-angled snow slope. But the snow was wholly unstable. 'It was like powdery sugar, completely unconsolidated to a great depth,' Mo says. 'If you'd jumped into it, you'd have gone in up to your face and still not have packed anything down under your feet. It could have broken off anywhere at any moment and there was no way of belaying ourselves. So we turned back.' The expedition had been financed by a provincial newspaper group which was 'very upset', Mo says. 'They wanted either the summit or a death. Anything in between was a failure, as far as they were concerned. I had a talk with them after we got back and when they hinted at this I lost my rag. I said, "If you can't trust the judgement of the people you've given money to, you shouldn't have backed them in the first place." '

This death-or-glory attitude of sponsors and the media is utterly at odds with Mo's view of climbing as an anarchic pastime that is fun to do. 'There's nothing nicer than climbers you respect saying, "That was a good effort," ' he says. 'But what's pleasant about the general public saying, "He's a great mountaineer"? It means nothing because they don't know what a great mountaineer is.' If you ask Mo to define 'good mountaineer' he quotes the late Don Whillans, a superlative climber who helped Joe Brown to transform the standards of British rock climbing and died in bed in 1985: 'A good one is a live one.'

Mo himself says that his ambition is to die at the age of eighty-six, shot by an outraged husband, and then to have his ashes flushed down the whistling loo at the Alpine Club in South Audley Street. 'I've got a real, healthy respect for falling off, probably because I started climbing in the 1950s, when protection was rudimentary,' he says. 'Even with modern gear, I can't get myself into the state of mind when I feel I can afford to fall off. That means I never climb at my maximum. If I get into a position where I think I might come off, I retreat or smack in a peg or stand in a sling. I don't think it's necessary to go flying one hundred and fifty feet through the air in order to prove that the move I'm trying to do is too hard for me. No one ever thinks he's going to die on a route; even the crazies imagine they've calculated the risk and are going to get away with it. But when you start pushing, so that your safety margin becomes a fine edge, big things can go wrong. I like to leave a really thick edge. For me, my safety margin is my strength. It's not that I train like these dedicated modern lads who don't drink or smoke and spend hours each day on climbing walls. I'm too old for that stuff and, anyway, half my climbing life has always been in the pub. But I'm lucky–I'm naturally strong. Joe Brown has this lovely, relaxed way of climbing, of conserving energy, and when I'm on a route with him he's always telling me to relax. I say, "That's the last thing I want to do!'' He reckons that if someone dived down and hung on my legs while I was climbing I still wouldn't budge. But the strength that keeps me plastered there is my safety margin and I like to think there's loads left over. Of course, I've had epics on the hills, but I've never deliberately decided to risk one. On the contrary, I've had epics through not risking things. You can have them easily enough without jumping into them, and every time I've overstepped the limit I've been choked off with myself because I think it's a kind of selfishness. It's the easiest thing in the world to snuff it on a mountain, and the higher you get the easier it is. But I don't think any hill is remotely worth it. No mountain is that important to me. Important, sure. But not that important.'

In climbing parlance, an epic is a near-disaster that ends happily and makes a good story afterwards. It is also a concept that varies from climber to climber. That night out on the Cima Grande registered very high on my epic scale and hardly at all on Mo's. From the Dolomites, he went straight on to Chamonix, and within a few days was having another hard time – on the Grand Capucin with an unfit partner, who kept passing out on the stances. The next year, 1965, he climbed, without incident, what were then two of the hardest climbs in Europe – the Phillip-Flamm on the Civetta and the Bonatti Pillar on Mont Blanc – and then was caught in a white-out on the South Face of the Géant, during which he rescued two lost, panicky and ungrateful Germans ('when we got them to the Torino hut they didn't even say thank you'). In 1966, on the Brenva, he and his partner waited to help some less experienced climbers and were caught in a three-day storm, during which one of the climbers died of exposure and Mo was so badly frost-bitten in the feet that he had to spend weeks in a hyperbaric tank. 'In those days, I assumed that every route you did in the Alps was an epic,' he says. 'Since I had one every time, I supposed everybody else did. Then I began to hear people saying, "Such-and-such is a nice route." And their knuckles weren't ripped to shreds and their eyes weren't out on stalks like chapel hat-pegs, so I began to realize I was doing something wrong.'

Part of what he was doing wrong had to do precisely with what he was doing right. To a degree that seems positively unhinged to the outsider, Mo, like all serious mountaineers, is willing to accept any kind of hardship as part of the normal day's work. Bad rock, bad weather, bad food, freezing bivouacs on stony ledges at the foot of nasty-looking faces or suspended from pitons halfway up them – all that is taken for granted, and is even reckoned, by some, to add to the enjoyment. (My own preference for warm rock, warm food and a warm bed – as well as my plain lack of ability – ensured that I would never make the big time in mountaineering.) Mo also had a realistic understanding of how much discomfort the human body can withstand. When I imagined we were going to freeze to death, he figured, correctly, that we were in for nothing more than a cold and uncomfortable night. But we were lucky on two counts: the route was relatively short and the weather cleared. The following year and the year after that–on the Géant and the Brenva–he was less lucky. At which point it became clear that his thick edge was someone else's thin.

One way of avoiding this predicament would have been to have climbed exclusively with people who were in his own league in terms of strength and technical ability. But because he is a sociable man with a wide range of friends, that would have gone against the pleasure principle by which he has always regulated his climbing life. 'Whenever I organize a trip, I want to go with my mates,' he says. 'When the hot young climbers pick a team they invariably go for track record and technical expertise, rather than for the people themselves. So if they make the summit they get a headline in *Mountain*, and that's it–it's over. But if you've been on a trip with great blokes, you remember it for years and years. Even in Britain, I don't climb with people I don't know because I don't get any pleasure from it. It's just going climbing. Of course, as you get older you kid yourself that it's not the hardness of the route that matters but the people, the feelings. You make any excuse rather than say that the big thing is to do the hardest routes you are capable of with people you like. So in a way there's more to it than pleasure. I can go up the Llanberis Pass and do a route I've done fifty times before with someone I like, and really enjoy myself. Then I come back home and forget all about it –it's just been a nice day out. But if I go out and do something that taxes me with a mate I get on well with, I come back and I savour it. I remember the

moves, what the other bloke said – all the little details –
for years after. It's the degree of commitment you put
yourself to with someone else that defines what you get
out of it afterwards. That's what climbing is all about
for me.'

One of Mo's elementary precautions against unnec-
essary epics was to make sure that he and his partners
were always properly equipped, and he became a stickler
for good gear long before he began to manufacture it
himself. I have come to dread the moment when he
sorts contemptuously through my rucksack and shames
me into throwing away slings and carabiners – and even,
once, a rope – to which I have become unreasonably
attached over the years. His self-propelled lip lifts at one
corner and curls down at the other, his eyes become slits,
his vowels shorten: 'I wouldn't climb upstairs with this
stuff,' he says.

With fifteen years of practice, he has become an
expert on how to equip an expedition, but his first
attempt – for El Toro – was a triumph of over-organiz-
ation and excess: three tons of gear and food for a mere
six people – 'enough to feed the Brigade of Guards
for half a year', he says. That first expedition had
other excesses, peculiar to Mo. Because his slipped discs
had not yet cured themselves, he took with him – and
swallowed – 1,000 codeine to dull the pain in his back;
he also spent the whole time on the mountain strapped
up in a whalebone corset. On the walk back through
the foothills he bought an old skull from an Indian
– it seemed, at the time, an appropriate memento of

the trip. When he changed planes at Miami airport a burly woman customs officer pulled the skull from his rucksack and then, with infinite distaste, the filthy corset. She arranged the two ghastly exhibits carefully on the table in front of her and shouted to a colleague, 'Hey, Chuck, we got ourselves a kink!'

4
Tyn-y-Ffynnon

That was in 1970, and by then Mo's reputation as a wild man–or even as a kink–had modified considerably. He had behind him eight Alpine seasons of increasingly impressive routes; he had finished the three-year college course and one year of practical training that qualified him as a teacher; and for two years he had been in a business partnership with Joe Brown. Brown's suggestion that they team up to produce safety helmets had come in 1968, at more or less the same moment that Mo was offered what seemed the ideal teaching job–chief instructor at an Outdoor Pursuits centre in mid-Wales. But when it came to choosing between steady work–with paid holidays and a pension at the end of the long tunnel–and private enterprise with a mate, there was no contest: 'I thought, it's more risky, but it sounds like more fun.'

By then, Mo was already married for a second time. His first marriage, in February 1964, had lasted ten months. His second, to Jackie, whom he met while they were both students at Coventry College of Education, is still going strong after twenty years. The popular image of a mountaineer's wife is probably like that of a frontier woman: large-boned, large-bosomed, leathery and patient. Jackie Anthoine is small, slim and shapely. She has a soft face, big eyes, a mass of curly brown hair, and in social situations she affects a giggly, slightly put-upon manner more appropriate to Blondie than to *Shane*. In other words, she looks like the kind of young woman who would be more at home on a Mediterranean beach than in an Alpine climbing hut, except that she carries no fat and has the biceps and hard legs of an Olympic gymnast. She also has many of the gymnast's gifts. She is now in her early forties and the mother of two small children, but shortly before the first of them was born she was starring in a BBC outside television broadcast that entailed her following Joe Brown up an exceptionally difficult climb in the Scottish Highlands, and not long before that I watched her demonstrate to my two children how to make an upside-down human arch out of yourself. 'It's dead easy,' she said. 'Put your legs apart, then bend over backwards slowly.' And she did: her spine curved, her legs strained, she put her hands flat on the floor behind her, then stayed like that, her hair hanging down to the floor, while her face gradually turned beet red. My daughter, then seven years old, a keen ballet dancer and as flexible as rubber, managed the feat with difficulty. Her ten-year-old brother – also no slouch – ended up flat on his back with the wind knocked out of him and a bruised backside.

When Jackie and Mo first met, she had never climbed and he was not sure he wanted her to. He says, 'I've seen so many women hanging around the climbing scene, bored, hating it, pretending to be keen. I didn't want

to add to the number.' He did his best to discourage
Jackie by taking her, for her first route, up a climb called
Munich–an exposed and relatively hard VS on Tryfan.
To his dismay, she romped up it and asked for more.
He let the matter rest for a week, and then took her
on to Clogwyn du'r Arddu, the most forbidding of all
Welsh crags, on which no route is easier than VS and all
are two or three times longer than most Welsh climbs.
'We did Longland's, Chimney and Curving Crack,' he
says. 'It's the only time I've ever done three routes on
Clog in one day. We finished up Curving'–so named
because it follows, very strenuously, a long, curving and
largely overhanging crack up the East Buttress–'and
she was quite knackered. And so was I, so I reckoned
it would put her off. Far from it. She thought it was
great. We've climbed together a lot since then. She's
very good at altitude and incredibly resilient. She always
carries more than I do on the hill.'

In the Alps, they became famous not only because
she followed him up hard climbs more easily and in
better style than many male climbers but also because
on the long slog up to the high huts–always the most
dismal part of Alpine climbing–it was invariably she
who carried the heavier sack. In the days before the
women's movement, this was considered eccentric on
her part and not proper on his. Climbing wives tended
to be indignant on her behalf, while climbing husbands
reacted with a kind of wistfulness, compounded of secret
admiration and simple disbelief at Mo's ability to get
away with it. To both, his standard response was, 'If

she can bear it, she can carry it!' The simple truth was that neither of them was much interested in coddling or being coddled. Also, they made each other laugh.

They needed to in order to cope with the one continuing epic of their married life: their house. It is called Tyn-y-Ffynnon – Welsh for 'the house by the well' – and when they moved there in 1966 the ancient holy well was the only thing on the property in working order. The house itself was a ruin: four walls of rough rhyolite blocks, some of them fallen; no roof, no doors, no windows. The earth floor was eighteen inches deep in sheep droppings and an eight-foot tree grew in the centre of what is now the living-room. Behind the main building was a slightly less tumbledown cow barn where they camped out on their weekends from college, cooking on a Primus stove and getting their water from the well. Their annual rent for this palace was £25; in 1968, they borrowed £600 from Jackie's father and bought the freehold. Because they were more or less penniless, they did the building work themselves, very slowly, driving up on Friday nights with the bag or two of cement they could afford that week and solemnly following the instructions in *The Reader's Digest Complete Do-It-Yourself Manual*. It took them six to eight months to get a roof on and to put in a floor, a temporary kitchen and a bathroom.

Mo now talks about those chaotic first years like a man waking gratefully from a nightmare: 'Forever knee-deep in filth, never seeming to finish anything. But that's what it's like being young. Now I'm older

I couldn't even contemplate it. But it seemed perfectly all right at the time.'

Rock climbing is essentially a lazy man's activity: concentrated bursts of effort on the rock face alternate with long rests on the stances when you lie back, smoke, admire the view, or mutter at the rain. As a result, climbers are strong on watching other people work and the Anthoines' struggle to make Tyn-y-Ffynnon habitable became a long-standing attraction in the Llanberis Pass. Jackie was the star of the show as she shovelled sand into the cement-mixer or wrestled with wheelbarrows full of the boulders Mo was laboriously excavating from the house. Her cheerful, shapely, seemingly slight figure manhandling gigantic loads was a permanent source of astonishment to everyone who stopped by for a brew. (She also took time off to light the Primus, boil the kettle and make the tea.) Mo called her, tenderly, 'the only cement-mixer that runs on a handful of muesli a day'.

Boulders are a natural part of the terrain in a mountainous area like Snowdonia, and, as the house slowly emerged from the ruins, they became Mo's greatest tribulation. The climax came when he was finishing the room that was to be their bedroom. The roof was on, the floor was laid, the new window-frames were in place when Jackie decided the doorway was in the wrong position. Mo tried to argue, realized he wasn't going to win and acceded wearily. This is what happened; Mo talking: 'I found a piece of chalk, drew the shape of the door on the wall where she wanted it and began chipping away with a cold chisel. I started from the top, knocked the boulders out, put in a timber prop to support the weight above and worked my way down. When I got to within nine inches of the floor I found a little hump sticking up. I started going along it with the chisel and discovered it was the biggest boulder in the whole cottage: seven feet long, two and a half feet wide, two and a half feet deep. It weighed two tons and it was right in the bedroom! It was too big to go out of the doors and I'd just put the windows in, so what was I to do? Since there were a couple of other smaller boulders in the room, I decided the best solution was to winch the things out. So I knocked out the nice new window, angled two pitch pine beams up to it, drilled a couple of expansion bolts into the boulder, joined them up with slings and hooked them to a cable. Then I borrowed a hand winch, anchored it to a tree in the field outside and attached the cable to it. The winch worked like a windlass and gradually Joe Brown and I wound the boulders up these two inclined pieces of timber. I had a little dumper truck parked right outside, its skip level with the window's edge, so the boulders would come up and plop straight into it. When we got the big one in it was so heavy that every time I put the brakes on the truck the back wheels came off the ground! I drove off to dump it where they were building the dam on Llyn Padarn. It was a Sunday, a summer evening, about six o'clock, and the locals were just coming out of chapel. One of them was a bloke who worked for me in the helmet factory. As I drove past – stripped to the waist, covered in sweat and filth, the diesel engine going "bb...bb...bb...bb..." –I called out, "Hello, Will." He wouldn't even look at me. He just gripped his bible and stared at the ground and pretended I didn't exist. They take their Sundays seriously in Wales! When I got back to the cottage Joe was sitting in the field, pale as a ghost. He'd started to winch out another boulder on his own and, to save time, had put in just one bolt. As he was winching away, he heard a muffled bang and something came whooing past his face. It was the end of the cable with a big metal hook on it. The bolt had sheered and the cable had come whistling straight through the window, shaved his face and ended right back in the field. Another few inches and it would have taken his head off! He put three bolts in the next boulder! It's always the daft things that hurt you, isn't it?'

The other, lesser, continuing epic was that of the bathroom which has now been put in, taken out and put in again three times. On the first occasion, Mo had *The Reader's Digest Complete Do-It-Yourself Manual* open at page 292, 'Fitting and cleaning baths', and was about to set to work when Joe Brown arrived with Nat Allen, another well-known climber. Since both Joe and Nat had begun their working lives as plumbers, they took over. Mo again: 'Joe said, "It needs to be offset. Pull this over here. Do this. Do that." I had two trained plumbers telling me how to install a bath and in the end the water ran uphill!' Because of that small miscalculation, an airlock formed in the wastepipe and the only way to empty the bath was to put your head underwater and blow down the plughole. On one occasion, when Mo took a bath without locking the door, someone came in and found him with his backside in the air and his head burrowing down the wastehole under six inches of soapy water, like Tolstoy's hysterical wife trying to drown herself in the shallow pond at Yasnaya Polyana. The present bathroom works perfectly.

The present house, too, is one of the grandest in the area. In 1985, to cope with a growing family and a growing preference – when off the hill – for a comfortable life, Mo made one final, massive push and added a second storey that provided three extra bedrooms – one small, two very large – extra storage space for climbing gear, and a second (level) bathroom. The upper rooms are high and light and airy under a pitched roof that looks like an inverted tick – short and steep at the front, a long slope at the back. The roof is grey slate, the stone walls are painted white, and the overall effect is of a stately Swiss chalet stripped of its hearts-and-flowers woodwork and redone in enduring Welsh stone. The cow barn out back, where the Anthoines had originally camped out, has also been added to and is now an elegant two-roomed house for guests which they refer to, dismissively, as 'the mini-hut'. 'What I like about building my own house,' says Mo, 'is that I can look at it and know it will still be there in a hundred years' time.'

5
Road to Roraima

The 1970 attempt on El Toro gave Mo a taste for expeditions, because they combine the pleasures and trials of ordinary mountaineering with a wider style of adventure – fun with his mates with the added attractions of remote places and different cultures. In 1972 he joined what was grandly called an Anglo-American expedition ('The American side was one nineteen-year-old called Larry Derby and an English lad, Ian Wade, who was living in the States,' he says) and returned to South America where they put up a new and very difficult route on Mount Fitzroy in Patagonia, an area famous for its unspeakable weather and hundred-mile-an-hour winds which have been known to perform an Alpine version of the Indian rope trick: they blow 140-foot lengths of full-weight eleven-millimetre Perlon rope vertically into the air.

The next year it was South America again, this time with an all-star team – it included Joe Brown, Don Whillans and Hamish MacInnes – sponsored by the *Observer* for what that normally restrained newspaper chose to call a 'climb to the Lost World'. The catchy name came from a Conan Doyle novel in which intrepid Edwardian explorers discover a pocket of palaeozoic prehistory–complete with monsters–surviving on the summit of Mount Roraima, a 9,000-feet-high rock plateau with a prow that rises 1,700 feet vertically out of the jungle at the point where Guyana, Venezuela and Brazil meet.

Back in England, even I, who have never suffered from expedition fever, was envious; it sounded to me less like a mountaineering expedition than a kind of tropical Hope-Crosby road film, with every expectation of meeting Dorothy Lamour along the way. In reality, it was one of the hardest trips any of them had ever been on, and the first indication of what might be in store came the evening before they left, when the Anthoines were staying at my home in London. My wife had put the roast lamb on the table, I was carving, my son was pouring drinks, when Hamish MacInnes telephoned from Scotland. He had just heard that the jungle at the base of Roraima was infested by vampire bats and the bats were rabid. Inoculation against their bite was possible but it entailed a series of painful jabs in the stomach. Mo's only comment was, 'Thank God we're too late for that.' He left the next morning as planned.

As it turned out, the vampire bats were not a problem, nor were the spiders as big as dinner plates. The problem was the mountain itself. On the Guyana side, it launches out into the surrounding jungle like a great ship but, because the constant tropical rain makes waterfalls of the vertical faces, the only way to get up the thing without drowning was to climb the hugely overhanging prow. The rock was a sandstone quartzite so compacted that long sections of it were blank, without cracks or other weaknesses–holds, for instance–and could be climbed only by bolting, a laborious and primitive procedure that entails hammering a hole into the rock with a star drill and then screwing in an expansion bolt. To insert twelve bolts a day, hammering at full stretch while dangling in étriers from an overhanging wall, is about as attractive a way of passing the time as cleaning out the Augean stables. And on Roraima, the rock overhung from top to bottom, sometimes by as much as thirty feet in a single 120-foot pitch. There were tiny ledges on the way but, because this was the tropics, great moustaches of vegetation hung from them. This meant that on the last six feet of many of the pitches the leader had to chop his way with his piton hammer through overhanging earth and plants, while what Mo called 'weird beasties' dropped down his neck and chest. The 'beasties' were a variety of oversized insects, most of them shaped like earth-moving machines and many so exotic that they had never been classified by entomologists.

Despite the perpetual rain that bucketed down beyond the overhangs, the only drinkable water on the route was the moisture that collected in pitcher plants on two insect-infested but relatively spacious ledges: one, christened 'Tarantula Terrace', near the bottom, the other 800 feet up. So at the end of each day the climbers had to abseil down over the huge overhangs like spiders letting themselves down on their own threads. They would then leave the ropes in place and jumar all the way up again to their previous high point the next morning. (A jumar is a metal clamp with nylon loops attached to it to stand in and hold; it moves easily upwards and locks when downward pressure is applied.) Jumarring is always a boring and exhausting process, but when it has to be repeated day after day on ropes that have begun to fray on the sharp edges of rock it can, as Mo mildly put it, 'prey on your mind a bit'. In fact, it preyed on their minds for over three weeks while they laboured – soaked, filthy and unnerved – up and down the face on increasingly frayed ropes to the summit. During one dark night of their collective souls, when all of them had run out of reasons for being there, Mo came up with a comforting thought: 'Well,' he said, 'it's better than de-scaling a boiler in Sheffield.'

For Mo, another consolation was that he learned from the expedition's Indian guides about how to survive in the jungle. But even that was not quite what he had expected. One day he asked one of the Indians how to light a fire when you are lost in the rain forest. This is what happened: 'He showed me this particular tree that they use. He lopped off a branch with his machete, sharpened one end into a point, stuck it in the ground, then started chopping delicately downwards with his machete in very fine slices, all the way around, so that it ended up looking like a shaving brush. When you light the underside, there is so much surface area and so little wood that it will catch fire quickly. He said, "You do all this; you put sticks round her; then" – dramatic pause – "you tip paraffin over her!" '

6
Feeding the Rat

Mo has a vivid and precise expression for what drives him – and most other climbers – to court discomfort; he calls it 'feeding the rat'. When he got back from Roraima, his rat was well and truly fed, but he himself looked thinner and more wasted than I had ever seen him. Even so, within a few months he was brooding about another expedition, but this time Jackie complained strenuously about being left behind. So they decided to concoct a private trip with three friends – Bill Barker, Malcolm Howells and Ian Campbell – to the Langtang Himalaya, an area west of Everest and about a dozen miles from Xixabangma, the only mountain in China that is over 8,000 metres high. To save money, they drove overland from Wales to Kathmandu, via Afghanistan, and got a trekking permit rather than a permit for a full-scale expedition. But that did not stop them, in Mo's words, 'knocking off a little rock column and climbing a small peak – about twenty-one thousand, I think it was. It was hard work and a long way to walk, but it was nice.' Barker, Howells and Campbell climbed the peak first, then Mo and Jackie climbed it together, both of them a little apprehensive about how they would perform at altitude, although Mo had already been up to

20,000 feet on El Toro. As it turned out, 'Jackie went like a steam engine' and Mo also found that he had no problems.

That was in 1974, and every summer from then until 1983 he returned to the highest of all the mountain ranges, either to the Himalayas or the Karakoram. Most of these expeditions have been low-key affairs, largely financed by the climbers themselves – occasionally with a little help from the Mount Everest Foundation and the British Mountaineering Council – but without media coverage and often not even reported in the trade papers – *Mountain*, *High* and *Climber* – unless they made the summit. They were less like expeditions as the general public conceives of them than like extended versions of Mo's ideal of a day out with his mates.

The sole exception was in 1977, when Mo was invited to join an attempt on the Ogre, a 24,000-foot peak, which is the highest point in the Biafo glacier region of the Karakoram. The route was long, technically demanding – it involved steep granite and steep ice that would be hard even in the Alps, at half the altitude – and it had already defeated two British and two Japanese teams in the previous six years. In other words, it was a perfect way of feeding the rat.

Although Mo knew and liked the other five members of the team, only one – Clive Rowlands – was a close friend, and two of them – Chris Bonington and Doug Scott – were full-time professional mountaineers. Bonington is probably the one British climber whose name is known to complete outsiders: he has written a number of books and organized several well-publicized expeditions to famous mountains, such as Everest and Annapurna; he appears regularly on television and has had his face in newspaper advertisements endorsing all kinds of non-mountaineering products. Scott, a huge, bearded man of phenomenal strength, is less well known and not at all part of the establishment–politically, he professes to be an anarchist–but he has made many spectacular first ascents and he finances his climbing from the lecture circuit. Every climber–professional and non-professional alike–wants to get to the top of whatever route he is on, however small; that is what the game is about. For the professional, however, the summit has a special, personal intensity that non-professionals can never quite generate: it is, quite simply, his material. On the Ogre, they got their material with a vengeance, although the summit was the least part of it.

By the time it came to the final push, the original party of six had been reduced to four: Paul (Tut) Braithwaite had been injured by a rockfall; Nick Estcourt was exhausted by a preliminary and unsuccessful bid for the top with Bonington. That left Scott, Bonington, Clive Rowlands and Mo on the mountain, with the other two at Base Camp, on the glacier, far below.

The Ogre has two summits, the West and the Main–which is 200 feet higher–connected by a long, jagged ridge. On 12 July, Mo and Rowlands led up to the West Summit, then the four climbers spent the night in an ice-cave that they had dug on the South-East

Face, just below the ridge. The next morning, Scott and Bonington traversed below the ridge and began to climb the steep and difficult rocks of the Main Summit tower. Because Mo was filming the climb for the BBC, the plan was for him and Rowlands to wait at the cave for an hour, taking pictures and keeping warm, then to follow the others to the top. But when they reached the base of the final tower they found that Bonington, gripped by summit fever, had omitted to leave the gear in place. Although they themselves were carrying no extra equipment, they managed to free-climb two hard pitches, until they were in shouting distance of the others. At that point, Scott had reached an area of blank rock at the top of a steep wall and was in the process of penduluming across to a crack that led to easier summit rocks. (The pendulum is a way of moving sideways across holdless rock. The climber attaches the rope to the highest point he can reach, then lowers himself and swings back and forth, literally running across the rock face, until he has gathered enough momentum to reach another line of weakness. It is a technique sometimes needed on hard rock climbs in places like Yosemite – the Nose on El Capitan involves a particularly spectacular pendulum – but is rarely used at high altitude.) Bonington called down to say that this was the last serious pitch and when they were up it he would drop the others a rope. But by then there were only two hours of daylight left, so Mo and Rowlands decided, very reluctantly, to retreat to the ice-cave and make their own summit bid the next day.

Scott and Bonington reached the top, took the obliga-
tory photographs, then started back down. By the time
they reached the top of the steep pendulum pitch, the
light had almost gone. Scott abseiled down it, steadily
pushing himself across the face in order to reach the
piton from which he had pendulumed on the way up.

Later, in an article in *Mountain*, he described what
happened next: 'I leaned across to fix myself on to a
peg, pressing myself over with my feet. I stepped my
right foot up against the wall, but, in the gathering
darkness, unwittingly placed it on a veneer of water
ice. Suddenly my foot shot off and I found myself
swinging away into the gloom, clutching the end of
the rope. I couldn't imagine why the swing was going
on and on. I had not realized how far left of the abseil
sling I was. All the time I was swinging a little
exclamation of awe, surprise and fear was coming out
from inside me, audible to Mo some 2,000 feet away
in the snow-cave. And then the swing and the cry
ended as I slammed into the opposite side of the
gully.'

The impact broke both his ankles. Bonington abseiled
down to him. But by then it was dark. They abseiled
farther down, to a large patch of snow – Scott keeping
his back to the rock when he abseiled and moving, when
he had to walk, on his knees – where they bivouacked
miserably.

Mo and Rowlands had watched the accident, appalled,
from the ice-cave, knowing there was nothing they
could do in the dark. At dawn, Mo left Rowlands in

the cave to brew tea while he traversed across to help the others. Scott, on his knees, greeted him cheerfully, saying, 'I'll just nip back to the snow-hole, youth.' Then he asked, apparently quite seriously, 'Are you and Clive going to the top?'

The printable part of Mo's answer was, 'I think we may have a bit of a job on here.'

The major problem was that they were about 9,000 vertical feet above their base camp, and much of the route had been diagonal. Scott had relatively no trouble abseiling downward, and, because of his phenomenal strength, could manage to haul himself upward. But on his knees, traversing – even downhill – was difficult and terribly painful. There was also a secondary problem: assuming that they would soon be heading back down the mountain, they had eaten up nearly all their food the evening before the summit bid.

Back at the ice-cave, they decided that, with the small amount of climbing gear they had left, their safest way off the mountain was to climb back to the top of the West Summit; from there it would be downhill most of the way, even though the downhill would involve a good deal of traversing. Until then, the weather, at least, had been perfect, but by the time they had made their plans clouds were rolling in – 'just like they always do in situations like this', Mo said – and by late afternoon it had started to snow fiercely. They ate the last of their food and spent an uneasy night trying to block the entrance of the ice-cave to prevent the snow from drifting in.

A blizzard blew all next day. At ten in the morning, Rowlands roped up and went out to try to force a way up to the West Summit. It took him an hour and a half to go fifty feet; when he came back into the cave his clothes were iced over and his hands were dead. An hour later, Mo went out to see what he could do. Although Rowlands had ploughed waist-deep through powder snow, there were no signs of his tracks. Mo made a mere thirty feet in the white-out and then gave up. He, too, had lost all sensation in his hands; it was so cold that his eyelids froze to his eyeballs. They spent the rest of the day in the cave, listening to the blizzard and struggling to keep the entrance clear.

The storm was still blowing the following morning, although the wind had eased a little. But, whatever the conditions, they had to move: their food was gone, they had only one gas canister left with which to melt snow for drinks, and they knew that at that altitude and in those conditions they would soon be too weak to move at all. Rowlands led the way, slowly kicking up the deep, steeply angled powder snow; then came Scott, on his knees, hauling himself up the rope with jumars; Mo, like a sheepdog, came behind him, while Bonington stayed in the ice-cave until the last moment, in case they had to retreat. On the final, steepest section to the West Summit, the powder was so deep that Scott, despite his strength, found that he was simply ploughing himself farther and farther in. So Mo climbed past him to help Rowlands pull, Bonington got behind to shove, and, between them, they hauled Scott to the top.

Later, when I asked Mo if he had thought they might not survive, considering the storm and Scott's injuries, he answered, 'It simply never occurred to me that we might die. Of course, I knew that if we stayed up there and did nothing, then, sure, we'd snuff it eventually, because no one was going to come and help us. But I thought that as long as we kept moving we'd survive. We were four tough blokes, and, fortunately, the toughest of us was the one who was injured. Perhaps it would have been different if it had been someone without Doug's physical strength who had broken his ankles. But Doug himself was quite cool about it and, although he was in pain, he never once complained. When we talked about it afterwards he told me that in his mind there was no way he was going to die—no way at all. He said he knew he was in good hands and he reckoned he was strong enough.'

In his subsequent account, Scott wrote: 'There was only one way for me to tackle a big, complex problem like that, and that was one day at a time, keeping the broad idea hovering around in my mind that I'd got to get to Base Camp, but each day thinking no further than that day's objective, confident that if each day's climbing was competently executed then the whole problem would eventually be solved.'

It was midday by the time they were all on the West Summit, and the storm was still howling. But the visibility had improved to about fifty yards, and at least there would be no more vertical uphill fights. Because Mo and Rowlands were not injured and had not had to bivouac at 23,500 feet, without food or equipment, they were clearly in better physical shape than the two others. So from there on Mo took over the lead, finding the route, fixing the belays and abseils, while Rowlands stayed with Scott to help him over the awkward bits, and Bonington brought up the rear. That day, their goal was a second ice-cave, about 1,000 feet below the West Summit. The abseils towards it were no great problem, but Mo was worried about a long, difficult traverse across steep ice immediately before the cave: because it was horizontal, there was no way for him to cross it without leading, and in the dreadful conditions that meant the possibility of falling off. 'Fortunately, it had been preying on my mind all the way down,' he said. 'I was so keyed up by the time I got to it that I just whistled across. It's amazing what fear and adrenalin will do!'

The night in the second ice-cave was as miserable as the others had been. They spent most of the time massaging each other's feet and cradling them in their laps in the hope of restoring the circulation. By next morning, the storm had still not slackened. Below them was a 1,000-foot rock pillar – the hardest section of the climb on the way up – and below that was Camp 3: two small tents, in which they hoped there might be food. So they set off, despite the blizzard and the sub-zero temperatures, on a whole day of abseiling with no possibility of shelter until they reached the tents. Halfway down, Bonington, bringing up the rear, shot off the end of an abseil rope, smashed into a boulder and broke two ribs, one of which damaged his lungs. 'Cold and getting colder, he had no alternative but to continue the descent,' Scott wrote. 'Mercifully, he did not at once start to experience the pain in his thorax that was to dog him later. It was a sorry little band that made the tents. Mo was the first and he had to re-erect them, as they were both flattened under three feet of snow.'

There was no food at Camp 3, but there were tea-bags, fuel, and, most important, a pound bag of sugar. So when they woke on the fifth morning after the accident to find that two more feet of snow had fallen during the night and the storm was raging more violently than ever, they decided to wait it out for one more day and hope that hot sweet drinks would restore a little energy.

Bonington was in a bad way, coughing continual-ly and bringing up an ominous-coloured phlegm. He grew worse as the day went on, and gradually became convinced that the pains in his throat and under his ribs were symptoms of pulmonary oedema – the occupational hazard of high-altitude mountaineering. If that was what he had, there was every chance that he might not survive unless he could get down the mountain quickly. The others listened critically to his coughs and wheezing, then tried to cheer him up by saying they couldn't hear the gurgling noises that are supposed to be characteristic of the illness. Bonington was not consoled.

In emergencies, Mo tends to give himself a hard time, while leaving his pals a good deal of elbow room for their idiosyncrasies. He has a shrewd and witty eye but does not hold other people's weaknesses against them. All that is part of his expedition philosophy, in which 'a trip with great blokes' wholly outranks getting to the top. Later, he described Bonington's predicament to me sympathetically: 'Chris knew that he'd done something to himself but he didn't know what. He just knew that he was deteriorating very rapidly. He also knew that if you get chest infections when you are high up anything can happen, because the altitude compounds the infections and accelerates the speed they work at, so you become very ill in a very short time. Doug knew what was wrong with *him*: he'd broken both his ankles. But Chris didn't have a clue. And it doesn't help you mentally when you're worried about what is going on inside yourself and have no idea what it is I felt quite sorry for him in that respect. But when you are in a survival situation you become a bit callous. The bloke's lying there next to you in his sleeping bag and you can hear him going, ''Aarrghh...aarrghh.'' It's awful, of course. But you're not an intensive-care nurse. You don't say, ''There, there.'' You say, ''Get a grip on yourself–you've got to do something about this.'' '

Bonington, among his other considerable gifts as a mountaineer, has prodigious reserves of fortitude. The question was how to tap them in his rapidly deteriorating condition. Mo keeps going by making fun of himself and his particular brand of humour is much like that of the Czechs, as the writer Vaclav Havel once described it: 'Here we tend to be...intensely conscious that anyone who takes himself seriously soon becomes ridiculous, while anyone who always manages to laugh at himself cannot be really ridiculous.' On Roraima, Mo had rallied everyone's spirits with a deflating joke. Bonington's version of de-scaling a boiler in Sheffield was different but equally effective. He is a graduate of Sandhurst, and his voice is usually loud and commanding. But by late afternoon on the fifth day of the storm, twenty-four hours of coughing had reduced it to a sandpaper whisper. He rolled over in his sleeping bag and croaked to Mo, 'We're going to make a fortune out of this.'

'How come?'

'The book!' said Bonington.

It was at that moment that Mo finally understood that he was not then and never had been a professional mountaineer.

The wind was still blowing the next morning, but the snow had stopped, and gradually the clouds rolled back and the sun appeared. It was now six days since the accident and they were still less than halfway down the mountain. They abseiled down to the West Col on fixed ropes they had left behind them on the ascent, then traversed across to their Camp 2, in the hope of finding food. Mo and Scott got there first, but all they could dig out from the snow was a packet of throat pastilles, one 'Tom and Jerry' nougat bar, and a waste bag containing some scraps of rice mixed with cigarette ash. They gobbled the grains of rice guiltily, then divided the rest and left half for the others.

Below them was a mile and a half of deep snow, angling gently down to the top of the final steep section before Advanced Base Camp. Halfway down, Mo stopped for a rest, and Scott caught him up and announced that he wanted to take his turn in front breaking the trail. Mo was carrying a larger sack than Scott, as well as a mass of slings and carabiners. 'As he crept past, I thought, if he's crawling, he can carry a bit more,' Mo said. 'Anyway, he won't notice. So I clipped the slings on to him. Unfortunately, Clive Rowlands was right behind me and he captured that on camera.'

They set up the tents above the fixed ropes on the last steep section. They were still 2,000 feet above Advanced Base and about 5,000 vertical feet and five miles distant from Base Camp. All of them were in bad shape, but, in Mo's words, 'When you realize you are only a day, or two at most, from people and food you're not all that worried. It's when you're on the top with nothing to eat that you feel a bit peckish.'

Because of the injured men, it was important to move quickly over the terrain below, so they agreed to lighten their sacks by abandoning everything that was not absolutely necessary: helmets, hardware, extra ropes and, when the night was over, the tents. But when Bonington decided to leave behind an expensive camera, Mo said, 'I'll have that,' and stuffed it swiftly into his sack before Chris could change his mind. His excuse later was: 'I thought, I've thrown everything else away – I've got room for one little luxury.'

At first light, he and Bonington set off down the fixed ropes, leaving Rowlands to shepherd Scott when the day warmed up. At the bottom of the steep section, they found that Advanced Base had been abandoned, so they headed straight on down, first for a mile over crevassed snow, then on down the long glacier – two and a half miles on ice, one mile over moraine. Scott said later that those last three and a half miles were, for him, the worst passage of all. He had three layers of clothing to protect his knees, and strips of plastic sleeping mat as well, but when he crawled into Base Camp at ten-thirty that night all the protection had worn away; his knees were numb and bloody and swollen to the size of melons.

Bonington was now near the end of his tether, coughing ominous yellow phlegm and nodding off whenever he paused for a rest. So as soon as they reached the relatively safe ground of the ice glacier, where the crevasses were visible, Mo left him behind and made a dash for Base Camp to rally help. But Base Camp, too, had been abandoned. Nick Estcourt had waited there for a week, with six porters, while the storm raged on the mountain. When the climbers had not appeared by the second morning of fine weather, he had given them up for dead and gone down to the nearest village, Askole, to organize a search party. He had, in fact, set off that same morning, 20 July, leaving behind a bleak note that began, 'If you get as far as reading this, then it presumably means that at least one of you is alive...' He had also left a one-pound canned fruit cake, fifty nougat bars, and whatever bits

and pieces he had been able to keep from the hungry
porters.

Mo took a quarter of the cake, a nougat bar and half
a packet of soup, left a note to say he was going on to
Askole, and set off immediately. It was by then nearly
five in the afternoon and he had already been going
for twelve hours. The distance to Askole was about
thirty-five miles – twenty-five to Korophon, where the
Biafo glacier ends, then ten along the bank of the Braldu
river. A couple of times, Mo fell asleep on his feet and
woke to find himself still walking. That unnerved him,
so he set himself a routine: sixty minutes walking, then
a five-minute cat-nap. He walked until midnight, when
the moon went down and he could no longer see where
he was going, then slept four or five hours, until first
light. He kept walking all the next day – sixty minutes
on, five minutes off – and was just past Korophon by
midnight. From there on, the ground was relatively flat.
But there was a rock step to negotiate and by the time
he reached it the moon was down again, so he slept
for another few hours. When he walked into Askole
at seven o'clock the next morning the first person he
saw was the headman of the village, whom he knew
from two previous expeditions to Trango, a mountain
in the same area. 'The Baltis don't normally show much
emotion,' Mo said. 'But when he saw me he did a sort
of vertical take-off into the air, then dashed up and
hugged me. Bloody hell, I thought. So I slogged on up
the street, very slowly, because it was uphill, and when
I came to the camp site there was Nick running towards

me. I've never seen such pleasure on a bloke's face. He was convinced we were all dead.'

Within a couple of hours, Estcourt and a dozen porters had set off for Base Camp. They made the long, uphill journey in just over twenty-four hours and brought Scott back down to Korophon on a stretcher, handling him as tenderly as a baby. Meanwhile, a runner had gone to Skardu, the nearest town of any size, and the authorities there radioed Rawalpindi for a helicopter to collect the injured men, one at a time, from Korophon. But even then the disasters were not quite over. Coming in to land, with Scott strapped to a stretcher, a rotor failed just as the chopper cleared the edge of the escarpment on which Skardu stands. The machine dropped twenty feet and crashed into the ground. No one was hurt, but if the failure had occurred ten seconds earlier they would have missed the escarpment and smashed like eggs. The worst casualty was Bonington, who had to wait a week in Askole for a second helicopter to arrive.

7
The Pleasure Principle

D escending a long, difficult mountain in a six-day blizzard, without food and with two broken ankles, was an act of extraordinary courage on the part of Doug Scott, and, back in England, it made the headlines. It even earned Scott a trophy from a London casino, the Victoria Sporting Club. However, he strenuously insisted that the rescue had been a team effort, and when the casino refused to allow all four climbers to accept the trophy together on TV, he turned it down. Without Scott's strength and uncomplaining endurance there would certainly not have been a happy ending to the epic. Even so, the happy ending, like the climb and the descent, was entirely a team effort. Right up until the last day of the ascent, the four of them had taken turns leading, and, but for Bonington's absent-mindedness, they would all have been on the top together. When the disaster occurred, it was Mo and Clive Rowlands who got the other two safely off the mountain. Rowlands forced the route back to the West Summit through waist-deep powder snow, and Mo then led the hazardous descent, finding the complicated route in the storm, clearing the fixed ropes of ice, fixing the belays and the abseils. Finally, it was Mo who made the hallucinatory forced march back to Askole.

Yet, between the rescue and the ensuing publicity, a curious conjuring trick took place: Mo and Rowlands effectively vanished from the story. Mountains do not normally make headlines; Everest apart, it is rare for them to rate more than two or three inches of an inner column on an inner page. The Ogre, however, and Scott's extraordinary feat of endurance were given the full media treatment. The *Sunday Times*, for instance, ran a big centre spread with a picture, a diagram and plenty of death-or-glory detail. But even there, Mo and Rowlands appeared merely as spear-carriers, while in the downmarket papers they appeared not at all. In part, this was an application of the old Fleet Street principle: big names make big copy. As someone remarked to me at the time, 'It wouldn't do to say that two of the most famous climbers in the country had been hauled off a mountain by a couple of unknowns.' And had the journalists bothered to follow up the story, they would probably not have been helped by either Mo or Rowlands, both of whom share a distaste for publicity. 'You're as famous as you want to make yourself,' Mo says. 'Doug and Chris have to be well known, because they need the cash if they're to climb all the time. They have no other sources of income apart from lectures and writing. I've got a business, so I can afford not to push myself into the limelight.'

As though to prove his point, he wrote a deadpan account of the climb for the *Alpine Journal*, the staidest of all the trade papers, in which he dealt with the descent from the West Summit to Base Camp in sonnet length, a mere fourteen lines that included his considered opinion of the whole grim week: 'Strangely enough it was not a frightening experience and, while not pleasurable, it certainly did not lack in excitement.' No mention of frostbite, no mention of his final two-day walk. It was one way to counteract media hype.

Even so, the Ogre proved to him again the truth he had learned six years before, after the expedition to El Toro: that there is an unbridgeable gap in expectations between the media and the climbers themselves. When he was invited to join an all-star expedition to K2 the following year, he said no.

Instead, he went with three close friends – Martin Boysen, Bill Barker, and Pete Minks – to attempt the West Face of Gasherbrum 4. In 1976, the year before the Ogre epic, Boysen and Mo had climbed Trango, an elegant, 20,000-foot rock spire in the Karakoram. 'From the top of Trango I'd looked up the Boltoro glacier and seen this great car park full of peaks,' Mo said. 'It's an amazing sight, the best collection of mountains in the world – beautiful peaks all of them. I thought, I must go up there. And the West Face of Gasherbrum was just mouthwatering.' In 1958, when the great Italian climber Walter Bonatti made the first ascent of Gasherbrum 4, by the East Ridge, he had peered down the 10,000-foot West Face and remarked with awe that maybe it was a route for the 1980s. By those lights, Mo and friends were ten years premature. They did not get up it, although they might have if Minks had not fallen and broken his ankle. The other three kept climbing and reached 23,000 feet – about 3,000 feet from the summit – before the size and steepness of the face, the rotten rock, technically difficult climbing and sheer exhaustion stopped them. As it turned out, Bonatti was right: the West Face was finally climbed in 1985 and is currently regarded as the hardest route in the Indian subcontinent.

The next year, 1979, Mo went to the usually mild Kishtwar area of Kashmir to attempt a relatively small, 22,000-foot peak called Brammah 2. But the weather was uncharacteristically dreadful and they got nowhere. For the next four years, he returned each season to Thalaysagar, a 23,000-foot peak in the Garwal Himalaya, near the Chinese border. Each time, the expeditions were small, unsponsored and made up exclusively of friends. Jackie went along on the first attempt and performed extremely well. This was her third major expedition. In 1978, she organized an all-women Karakoram team to climb Bakhor Das. Like Mo on the Ogre, she filmed it for the BBC; unlike Mo, she won their Mick Burke Award for the best adventure movie. Mo's comment was, 'Of course she won. I taught her all I know.' On the third attempt on Thalaysagar, in 1982, the old firm of Mo, Joe Brown, Bill Barker, Clive Rowlands and Malcolm Howells reached a point where there were only a couple of hundred feet of rock and then an easy snow ridge separating them from the summit. But Brown and Howells did a juggling act with a rucksack full of essential equipment and managed to drop it down the mountain. So, once again, they had to turn back. The following year, 1983, Mo and Brown returned alone, reckoning to climb their old fixed ropes quickly to their previous high point, and then finish the route off. But a huge snowstorm when they were just beginning put paid to that. Another party used the gear the 1982 expedition had left in place and bagged the peak during a fine spell later in 1983.

Although Mo's success-rate was fairly low in terms of summits reached, fourteen straight years of expeditions adds up to a formidable amount of high mountain experience. And between expeditions Mo put in several seasons of winter climbing in the French and Swiss Alps, where conditions are often even more dire than in the Himalayas. He also made two jaunts – in 1979 and 1980 – into the forests of Ecuador to look for Inca gold. He went with Brown, MacInnes, Boysen and Jackie, and they found no gold. But they discovered the remains of an Inca gold mine and explored mountainous jungle near the source of the River Napo, where not even the Indians had been.

Yet, since the Ogre, none of Mo's mountaineering expeditions has been blessed by sponsors or newspapers. He and his friends have gone to the remote ranges in the same way as they once took off in summer for the Alps: for a climbing holiday, providing their own gear, and paying their own way. It is a way of restoring amateur status to an increasingly professionalized activity and it follows naturally from Mo's belief in the pleasure principle: 'Expeditions are supposed to be enjoyable,' he says. 'Admittedly, they're bloody hard work and sometimes you get frightened, but primarily they should be fun. If there's publicity involved, then it may be that the climbers who need it will ride roughshod over the others, and everything gets sacrificed to the summit. Well, I don't think getting to the top is all that important. You can always have another go. The things you remember after a trip are not standing on the summit but what went on while you were on the route. The nicest feeling is to know that you are relying on someone else and he is relying absolutely on you. On Roraima, for instance, when Joe and I had been on the face umpteen days and were still only about halfway up, we came to a horrible section we called the Africa Flake. It was Joe's lead, but he just did a few feet and backed off. He said he was feeling nervy, the rock wasn't right and he had the sensation that the whole flake could prise away if he banged a peg in the wrong place. So I said I'd have a go. We'd taken turns leading up to that point, but I led the next three pitches up the flake. When I got to the top of the third pitch I was absolutely done in. I was on a hanging stance with not very good nut placements and a thousand feet of nothing below my boots. I was a bit gripped and wet through, and I was there for hours while Joe climbed towards me, clearing the gear out of the crack as he came. When he finally reached me, he started to belay. I said, "Would you lead the next pitch?" He could easily have answered, "I don't feel like leading. I'm soaked, I'm exhausted, I've had enough. Let's call it a day and go back down." But he didn't. He led the next pitch, which was bloody hard and dangerous, and I'm sure he only did it for me, because he knew I wanted to get up it. That kind of gesture is typical of a good expedition. You get extremes of selfishness and extremes of selflessness. The funny thing is, you tend to forgive the selfishness – as long as it's not too exaggerated – because everyone suffers a lot.'

For the outsider, the quotient of suffering seems so high that it is hard to imagine how any expedition to the Himalayas or Karakoram could be classified as fun. The mountains are simply too big, too high, too remote. For someone who has climbed only, say, in North Wales, the first trip to a relatively big range like the Alps involves a whole apprenticeship in hardship and exhaustion and the continual need to cope with objective dangers beyond your control: bad rock, avalanches, stonefalls, unreliable weather. But at least in the Alps there are towns and villages scattered throughout the valleys, and comfortable, well-maintained huts strategically placed among the mountains; in some areas there are even cable-cars to shorten the initial slog up from the valley. But in the highest ranges there are no conveniences at all, and all the other problems are magnified several times over by the huge scale of the mountains: approach marches measured in weeks, not hours, and routes measured in miles instead of feet. Added to that are the extreme cold and the debilitating effect of high altitude that reduces even the strongest to slow motion. There is also the more insidious debilitation of spending weeks on end in areas where nothing ever grows and there is only rock and snow and ice. And beyond all that hardship is the sheer squalor and drudgery of expedition life. Mo speaking: 'Some people find that they can't cope with things being so uncomfortable day after day. It just gets them down. And that, in fact, is how the average person reacts. Unfortunately, climbing is so élitist that when somebody reacts normally the others say, "He doesn't go well at altitude." But the truth is, people who do go well at altitude are a bit freaky. Your Boysens and Scotts who can perform on technically difficult rock very high up are exceptionally rare, because above twenty-odd thousand feet even easy rock feels extreme. And the ability to tolerate the perpetual squalor is equally freaky. Apart from his drive and his talents as a mountaineer, there are two good reasons why Bonington has an excellent Himalayan record: he can put up with any discomfort and he's an absolute Philistine as regards food–he thinks any old mulch is great as long as it's stuffed full of curry powder. Joe Brown is the same: if it's chilli-hot he'll eat it, whatever it is. On an expedition, being squalor-proof is as important as having stamina. For example, on Annapurna in 1970, Don Whillans spent five days in a tent, living on porridge and cigars. Most people would crack up in those conditions. I'm sure I would now– and Don, too, if he were still alive. It's not even that they crack up. They just think: I've had it; it's too uncomfortable; it's no pleasure; I didn't come out here not to enjoy myself. Well, I myself go out there with the idea that I'm not actually going to enjoy it at the time but I'm going to enjoy it afterwards. I'm going to enjoy the experience I've had with my mates on the hill. If you get to the top, so much the better. But that's not the point. And if you're expecting joy every day, forget it.'

8
Snowdon Mouldings

At home in Nant Peris, however, even before Mo put the second storey on the house, the standards of comfort had risen steadily as Snowdon Mouldings expanded. The Joe Brown helmet, designed by Joe and Mo in 1968, quickly established itself as the best you could buy and became standard wear in the climbing world. When the German Alpine Club tested sixteen different makes of helmet the Joe Brown came first easily in every category; in a British equipment test its shock-absorption ability was so good that the testing laboratory rechecked its own equipment because it did not believe the results. Mo, who is strong on climbers' gallows humour, produced a celebratory promotional T-shirt picturing a JB helmet on top of a vaguely human mess and a pair of boots; the caption read, 'Well, his head seems OK!' As early as 1971, the reputation of the helmet was so high that a Japanese distributor representing 2,500 retail outlets came to Mo with a huge order. But at that time the whole operation was just four people in a little cottage off Llanberis high street. To fill the Japanese order would have meant expanding considerably, and that might, eventually, have led to a large production capacity and not enough orders. So Mo persuaded himself that it made sound business sense to turn the Japanese order down. Certainly, it made sense in a more personal way. Mo's attitude to Snowdon Mouldings was rather like his attitude to his first job, as a climbing instructor at Ogwen Cottage: it was something he would do as long as it did not spoil his enjoyment of climbing. In other words, he wanted to run the business but not be run by it. Since then, JB helmets have been sold to climbers all over the world, as well as to NATO and the FBI, and Snowdon Mouldings has grown and grown, and Mo no longer thinks of getting out. But the principle still applies: climbing first, money second.

Yet this, too, makes a kind of business sense, for his mountaineering experience is continually being fed back into the products that finance it. On winter routes in the Alps and on difficult ice in the Karakoram, Mo several times found himself in trouble when an ice-piton broke or the shaft of his ice-axe snapped. So he designed a titanium ice-screw and an ice-axe with a fibreglass shaft, neither of which would break under any circumstances. Since there was no room to make them in the Llanberis cottage, he took over a disused church in the Scottish Highlands in 1975 and converted it into a factory. Although the new factory was more than 500 miles from his base in Wales, the place was beautiful and the winter climbing marvellous. He named the axe the Curver, because of its droop-nosed head, and he celebrated it with another T-shirt. This one had on its back an end-on picture of the head of the axe buried squarely between the wearer's shoulder-blades, and the

Previous page. 1 The Spigalo Giallo, one of the most beautiful of all Dolomite climbs. Mo and Al are the lower pair.

2 Showbiz. El Toro Expedition members modelling sheepskin coats for Morland's. Mo is kneeling in front, with Joe Brown behind him.

3 Mo on Roraima –
'better than de-scaling a
boiler in Sheffield'.

4 Jumaring is a
boring and
exhausting process.

5 Jackie on top of an unnamed peak in Langrang Himalaya – 'Jackie went like a steam engine'.

6 The Ogre Expedition members. *Left to right*: Clive Rowland, Chris Bonington, Nick Estcourt, Doug Scott, Paul Braithwaite and Mo. The Ogre is in the background on the left.

Mo as Rambo III

8 *The Mission. Left to right:* Hamish MacInnes, Mo and Joe Brown dressed to kill.

9 'I like adventures ... jungle travel, river travel, exploring ... places that are green on the map' – Mo fording the River Mulatas in the Upper Amazon Basin.

Opposite page: 10 'The Old Man sticks straight up out of the Atlantic like the admonishing finger of God.'

11 The Old Man of Hoy –
'not going anywhere but up'.

12 The Old Men of Hoy. *Left to right:* Paul Trower, Al and Mo.

slogan 'For better penetration'. On the front, the point of the axe emerged from what looked like a bleeding hole in the chest.

The Curver was a specialist tool that sold to con-noisseurs of hard ice, but never in sufficient numbers to make money. 'It was so expensive to produce that if I'd priced it realistically I would never have sold a single one,' Mo says. It was not until he designed a tent that the nature and scope of his business changed. 'On expeditions I got fed up with tents that weren't designed for high altitudes,' he says. 'Tents that leaked. Tents that fell down. Tents you couldn't put up in extreme conditions, or when you did get them up the poles broke and the whole thing collapsed on you. So I thought I'd make one the way I wanted it.' The result was the Limpet, a brilliant invention that can be pitched anywhere in a couple of minutes, needs no guy ropes, and is kept up and given its shape by flexible poles, like fishing rods, made of unbreakable pultruded glass and inserted into tubes in the fabric. The Limpet took two years to design and there are now five imitations of it on the market. (None of them, however, has the basic virtue of being self-supporting without guy ropes.) The Limpet also spawned a whole family of smaller Snowdon Mouldings variants: four types of mountain-bivouac bag, and an elder son called the Mini-Dome, which is a cross between a one-man tent and a bivvy bag. All of them, in suitable camouflage fabric, are now used by the British military. Although the Ministry of Defence has not yet given Snowdon Mouldings any official contracts, the gear sells widely at regimental level, particularly to the SAS and the Marines, and 1,000 Snowdon bivvy bags were used in the Falklands. The RAF tested the Limpet in the Norwegian snow and came back with five criticisms, all of which, Mo was delighted to tell them, had already been anticipated in the Mark III version. The RAF is now considering the tents for its helicopter survival packs.

The Limpet and its children are made from Gore-Tex, a miracle fabric that is impermeable to moisture from the outside yet lets out internal condensation. But Gore-Tex needs to be worked with special machinery: to remain waterproof, its seams have to be hot-air sealed with tape after they have been sewn. In order to justify the investment in the machines and to use up the spare capacity, the Anthoines began to manufacture waterproof clothing. Their method was the same as with their other products: they looked at what was on the market, decided where it needed improving, then made sure that their own workmanship was as good as possible. Like Mo, Jackie discovered that she was full of bright design ideas; she was also a stickler for quality, a perfectionist in whom shoddy work provoked un-Blondielike fury. At first she worked at home with a small team of sharply dragooned local women to help her cut and sew and seal, but the products soon overflowed the house. As well as the tents and bivvy bags, there was a whole range of waterproof jackets, overtrousers, snow gaiters and salopettes. And then Mo decided that no one had ever thought properly about gloves, although frost-bitten fingers are a major problem in the mountains. His solution was the SM Mitts, made of waterproof Gore-Tex outside, warm fibre pile inside. The Army is interested in those, too.

In 1982, Mo rented an old schoolhouse near Llanberis for Jackie and her team. Then, in 1984, he shut down the Highland church where the ice-axes were made, and bought a chapel in Llanberis. 'What I like about churches is they're just one room,' he says. This one is a big, nicely proportioned building, its outside rendered – by Mo – in waterproof white paint. In comparison with the little terraced houses around it, it seems grand and rather elegant. Mo himself converted it into a factory (in middle age, building seems to have become, for him, almost as addictive as climbing), first levelling the ground floor, which originally sloped like a theatre's, then putting in a separate floor to divide the building horizontally. The chapel had a high pitched roof, which made it expensive to heat. Mo solved the problem with a lower ceiling, which he suspended from steel straps bent over the massive roof beams and bolted to the ceiling joists. Like the floors below, the ceiling is 2,000 square feet in area but is level to within half an inch – a detail that pleases him.

The upper floor of the chapel is now the helmet factory, a clean, well-lit place permeated by the sharp chemical smell of styrene. ('It's like the Welsh rain,' Mo says. 'After a bit, you don't notice it.') Like pots in a pottery, the helmets are piled on shelves and distributed along the work benches in various stages of finish, from rough grey-white shells to brightly polished red, orange, blue and white. The helmet makers are all men, and to keep them happy and take their minds off the smell there is a life-size colour photograph of a reclining nude pinned along one wall. At the centre of the room is a glass-sided office for Mo's elder brother, Adrian, who is in charge of helmet production. Adrian is cheerful and easy-going, a shade taller than Mo but far slighter. He is a good organizer and very efficient, but although he occasionally goes out in the mountains he is not what Mo calls 'a specialist climber'. So he runs the day-to-day operation and leaves the technical development to his brother.

The lower floor, where the Gore-Tex products are made, is also bright and quiet, except for the hiss of compressed air from the generator that powers the machinery. But with sixteen machinists and cutters – most of them women, all of them locals – as well as Jackie and the manageress, Liz Crew, it seems crowded. Two huge tables run the length of the room; one is a cutting table, the other is lined with machines, and both were built by Mo. Thirty rolls of Gore-Tex – each costs £1,000 pounds – are stored on shelves beneath the cutting table, and along the edges of both the tables are boxes of gaiters, mittens and bivvy bags, and piles of jackets in plastic bags, each with the customer's name on it. A Mark III Limpet tent has been erected between the tables and every so often Mo goes up to it and peers and pulls and mutters to himself. Jackie and one of the machinists are in close consultation about a natty ski jacket and salopettes, in red and bright blue, that they are making specially for an eighteen-year-old local boy, Tim Lloyd, who is training for a place in the British Olympic ski team. At lunch-time, because it was just before Christmas when I saw the new factory, the workforce moved *en masse* to the nearest pub where they gossiped together like a large, giggly family, and Mo bought them undrinkable drinks–port and lemon, lager and blackcurrant, advocaat and lemonade. Within the hour they were all back at work, seemingly no worse for wear.

Later in the afternoon, Mo and I drove six miles through the rain to a small industrial estate just outside Caernarvon where, six months earlier, in May 1985, the Anthoines had opened another little factory, in partnership with a company called Cotswold Camping, to make clothes for the huntin', shootin' and fishin' set. The new firm was called Aquabeta and it produced hunters' jackets and overtrousers made of Gore-Tex instead of the traditional waxed cotton. Mo had a single, 1,000 square foot unit–as usual, he made the work benches and put in the electric wiring himself–but was about to expand into a similar unit next door, since Aquabeta had already begun to prosper. His neighbours on the estate were Laura Ashley and a couple of thriving computer companies, which might have been a sign for the future. (It wasn't. The partnership did not work out, and a year later Aquabeta had folded.)

I said it was strange that a man whose wardrobe was limited to jeans, T-shirts and half a suit should now be designing clothes. 'We're not in the fashion side of the market,' Mo answered. 'There are hundreds of manufacturers in it already and it's too cut-throat. Anyway, the only thing I know about fashion is that red goes with blue. I do my market research by going round the climbers' cafés and seeing which is the most popular colour. Climbers are a very conservative group and the colour, believe me, is navy blue. I think there is a lot of bull talked about design, especially the design of climbing gear. Ice climbing, for instance, is a real navvy's sport: for starters, you make your own holes. As for rock climbing – all you need are fingers like a chimpanzee's and you're away! Those are the facts you should bear in mind when you design gear. People are always asking, "Has it got this? Has it got that?" I think that as long as it fits and it's waterproof and it does the job it's intended for and it doesn't make you look like a sack of potatoes, it's OK. It's far too easy to overdesign. I once saw a tent with twenty-four zips in it, and now there are jackets with pockets sprinkled over them like plague spots. That sort of thing is OK for the cover of *Vogue*, not for the hills. The classic example of good design is Jean-Claude Killy's ski clothes: they're not flash, they're well made, they're perfect for the job, and they're expensive. I've never heard anyone complain about Killy gear, and in ten years' time it will still be in fashion. Those are the design principles I admire and I try to apply them to the things I produce. I test the gear myself in the mountains and I get feedback all the time from other climbers. The rest is quality control.

Essentially, design is a matter of thinking out simple solutions to basic problems. But you'd be surprised how little of that is done. I once watched a television programme about a single-handed Transatlantic sailing race. There was only one bloke who was properly organized – a sixty-year-old American, who kept dry and ate proper meals – and he was the guy who won. The others didn't have a clue. The whole lot of them were shivering and wet and hungry and miserable. All they needed was proper Gore-Tex clothing, and bivvy bags to protect their sleeping bags against condensation. But none of them had any of that, although their boats cost hundreds of thousands of pounds. If climbers were that slap-happy about looking after themselves in the mountains, they'd all be dead.'

Driving back to Nant Peris from Caernarvon, the wind had strengthened as the light failed, and there were white horses on Llyn Padarn. The clouds were down low over the Llanberis Pass, blotting out the peaks, and the rain moved like great billowing curtains between the edges of the lower cliffs. There were boisterous streams and little waterfalls lacing the hillsides where the day before there had been only rock and grass. Water, two inches deep, poured across the road, and the car trailed a plume of spray as it ploughed through. The stream that runs beside the path to Tyn-y-Ffynnon had overflowed its banks, and the water went over our shoes.

Inside the house, there was a blond child in front of a television set in both the downstairs living-rooms. Jo, aged three, was draped across a chair like an odalisque, watching a cartoon. Mo said, 'Ha!' and went into his monster routine, dragging one foot and gibbering ominously. Jo shrieked, then allowed herself to be tickled. In the other room, the ten-month-old Bill was perched at the back of his father's deep armchair, solemnly watching the early news. He held a can of beer in both hands and sipped at it with great concentration. The can was not open.

Upstairs, I sat on a packing case and watched Mo paint the dado of the second large bedroom – it would eventually be the children's – while we talked about his expedition plans for 1986. In June he and Joe Brown were going to Alaska to climb Mount McKinley twice – first by the ordinary route, up the West Buttress, then by the far harder Cassin Ridge, on the South Buttress. If that went well (it did), they would come back to Wales for a month to rest and fatten themselves up, then join a British attempt on the unclimbed North-East Ridge of Everest. The North-East Ridge is the one major problem left on Everest and its sting is in its tail: a series of difficult rock pillars at between 27,000 and 28,000 feet. The expedition would be large – sixteen climbers – but the Chinese had already announced that no porters would be available.

'That's not a problem,' said Mo. 'On the north side you can drive a lorry up to nineteen thousand; then you get on a yak and get off at twenty-one thousand.'

All the same, I said, weren't he and Joe getting a bit old to try the hardest route on Everest?

'No problem,' Mo replied. 'Joe says it'll be OK as long as we wrap up warm and get a good night's sleep.'

The prospect of Everest had already begun to do wonders for his training, which is not an aspect of climbing Mo normally indulges in. Two evenings a week, he was working out on an artificial climbing wall, and a third evening was spent doing gymnastics and stretching exercises. Each weekend, whatever the weather, he climbed. 'I don't get to go to Everest every year, so I might as well be as fit as I can,' he said. 'Then if I don't get up it, I can say, "It was too hard for me. I'm not up to that sort of thing." But at least I won't have the excuse of not being fit enough.' He used to claim–correctly–that most of his training was done in the pub. Now he was meeting his mates in the bar of the Royal Victoria only on Wednesdays and Fridays, when he limited himself to three pints of bitter, and on Saturdays, when he raised the ante to six pints if the action was good enough.

'How about smoking?' I asked.

'Funny you should mention it. I was just thinking about cigarettes. Then I thought, I'd better do something about it. So I'll have one.' He lit up, inhaled contentedly, and went back to his painting. After a while, he said, 'I'm giving up on January the ninth. January the first is too obvious, and, anyway, I never keep New Year resolutions.'

Once before, Mo had tried to give up smoking. He had made a bet with another climber who was also a heavy smoker: the first to light up would pay the other £250. On a Sunday morning six weeks later, the other climber turned up at Mo's house, looking sheepish. He shuffled his feet, scratched his neck, then pulled out his cheque book. He had been at a party the night before, he said. It was a good party and everyone else had been smoking. The temptation had been too much for him.

'Shall I give you the two-fifty?' he asked.

'Just give me a cigarette,' Mo replied.

On his second attempt, in January 1986, Mo held out for a mere two weeks.

9
The Mission

Once, when we were talking about two trips he had made to Ecuador to search for Inca gold, Mo gave me, in passing, a simple explanation of his version of the pleasure principle: 'I like adventures,' he said. 'And not just mountain adventures. I like jungle travel, river travel, exploring. I like going somewhere no one's ever been–places that are green on the map.' That taste for adventure, combined with his proven ability to look after himself in any circumstances, has produced for him a sideline which someone less busy might have parlayed into a profitable career: he acts as safety officer and climbing cameraman for the rock spectaculars that are popular on British television and for feature movies set in the mountains.

The Super 8 camera that Mo took with him to the Ogre did not win him the BBC's Mick Burke Award, but it did teach him something about shooting film, and gave him a taste for it. The Ogre was the supreme example of his dictum that when you get to the top you are only halfway there. On the Ogre, in fact, they were just beginning. Unfortunately, Mo used up his last reel of film shooting Scott and Bonington's arrival on the summit, and the epic descent went unrecorded.

After that, he took an 8-mm. camera along on all
his expeditions, trying to put on film what it really
feels like to the climbers to attempt a major peak.
'No film-maker has managed to capture the authentic
atmosphere of an expedition,' he says. 'It's a mixture
of excitement and apprehension–first the excitement
of a new mountain, then the grinding work and the
gradual build-up of pressure as you begin to realize how
easily avalanches can blow you away, or seracs can fall on
you, or you can drop down a crevasse. With luck, nothing
goes wrong, but the tension is always there, and it keeps
on building in everyone. Then, as soon as you've got
to the top or you've made the decision to retreat, this
hidden weight lifts, and people change. A professional
film crew has never caught any of that, because to film
people everything is new, and they don't really know
what they are looking for. All they do is film what
they see, but what they see is different from what the
climbers feel.'

His own elusive genuine expedition movie is still a
long way from completion. But the hundreds of feet of
film he has shot taught him lessons that the BBC put to
use when it needed a face cameraman who would dangle
down the cliff to film Joe Brown and Jackie climbing in
Glencoe. Mo talking: 'The one thing I remembered from
the Super 8 was not to try to be clever with the camera.
It's still the best rule: let the action take its course and
don't mess around; just frame it and keep it there;
don't start zooming and panning, because unless you
are a really good cameraman it's going to look awful.

Modern amateur cameras are ridiculously sophisticated compared with 16-mm. or 35-mm. cameras. They've got so many gimmicks – buttons for zoom, buttons for macro, buttons for everything – that it's tempting to be cute. Well, that was one temptation in life I managed to resist when I started filming for the Beeb. I just kept the camera steady and shot what the director, Mike Begg, wanted to see. If he said, "I want a close-up of Joe's hands," I'd get one, and I wouldn't move until I was told to. I didn't try anything arty-farty, and for Mike, I suspect, that was a relief. He also realized that the advantage of having a climber behind the camera is that he knows what's going to happen next. He knows where the hard move is. If someone is going to fall, the climber knows which hold he is going to fall from. The average cameraman doesn't know these things, so he could be looking at the skyline and doing a pretty-pretty at the critical moment. On top of that, if a non-climber is on awkward ground he's going to be worrying about himself rather than about his camerawork, while a climbing cameraman doesn't even notice the exposure.'

For Mo, being a cameraman was primarily a way of having extra climbing holidays with all expenses paid and a fee at the end. But in the film world one thing tends to lead to another. In 1981, Fred Zimmerman went out to Switzerland to shoot an Alpine movie starring Sean Connery and called *Five Days One Summer*. Mo was initially signed on as a safety officer, then he was put through a crash course on the Ariflex camera and given a contract as an assistant cameraman. He, Joe Brown and Hamish MacInnes spent most of the summer in the Swiss Alps, doctoring crevasses to make them safe for the film crew, manhandling equipment up and down rock faces and in and out of holes in the ice, acting as stand-ins in the climbing sequences, keeping a protective eye on everyone, and developing an expensive taste for champagne.

Mo also learned the subtleties of the Ariflex: he did the clapperboard and the loading, pulled the focus, cleaned the gate, changed the lenses and filters. But, according to the strict pecking order of the movie set, the one thing he could not do as an assistant cameraman was look through the lens. Mo, however, had other ideas. The chief cameraman was Arthur Wooster, a man who had a reputation, and had even won an award, for filming in dangerous locations. 'A smashing bloke', according to Mo. 'But a walking death-trap. He'd jump in anywhere, mainly through blind bloody ignorance.' For this reason, perhaps, Wooster was a sucker for the natural anarchy of the climbing world. 'I used to say, "Give us a look, Arthur," and the other assistant cameraman would groan in horror,' Mo said. 'But Arthur didn't mind. To him, I was just an outsider who wanted to learn how to shoot movies. So he was very helpful. He told me what to do and what not to do, how he framed his shots and why. He knew I wasn't after his job.'

One thing went on leading to another. There was more television work, including a series of Lakeland climbs presented by Chris Bonington, a film portrait

of Joe Brown, and a funny, irreverent programme
in which Brown and a startlingly overweight Don
Whillans reclimbed, thirty years on, one of their first
hard Welsh routes, Cemetery Gates. (At one point,
when the struggle with the greasy rock seemed about to
become too much for him, Whillans called out, 'Next
time you take me on a vertical stroll up memory lane,
make sure the rock's dry!') There was also another
feature film with Sean Connery, this one called *The
Highlander*. Then, in 1985, when David Puttnam and
Roland Joffé went out to the Iguazú Falls in Argentina
to film *The Mission*, they found they needed professional
help to cope with the cliffs and the river and the vast
waterfall itself. Once again, Brown, MacInnes and Mo
were sent for, and this time they did everything. They
acted as climbers, safety men, stuntmen, stand-ins, and
even engineered some of the special effects. They climbed
up through the waterfall both solo and with ropes, they
heaved cameras and canoes up cliff faces, and fixed ropes
from the river bank to a rock on the lip of the 250-foot
falls. Among their other duties, Brown doubled for
Robert de Niro and Mo for Jeremy Irons. ('That's
because I'm six foot two and blond!' Mo explained.)
Before the shooting was finished, the film men realized
that on a dangerous location, where nerve and ingenuity
are required, climbers are useful people to have around
even when there is not much climbing to be done.

The last postcard I received from Mo arrived in
September, 1987, and came from Israel. Once again he
was working on a movie, *Rambo III*, and once again he

was climbing vertical rock. This time his torso had been greased until it shone like a car in a showroom and he was standing in for Sylvester Stallone.

For the climbers themselves, movie work meant not just a free airfare to exotic places, with good pay and generous expenses, it also meant lavish helpings of Mo's favourite dish, adventures. 'What I like about the movies is that the best things always come suddenly, out of the blue,' he said. 'When you are sitting at home in Wales watching the rain, two years after the Falklands War, the last thing you'd expect is that one week later you'd be in Argentina – in one of the most beautiful places on earth – climbing waterfalls and dressed as a Jesuit priest.'

10
The Old Man of Hoy

W hen Mo and I first climbed together over twenty years ago, the ten-year difference in our ages did not seem to matter much. It mattered, of course, that he could get up climbs that I couldn't even start, but we solved that problem by keeping to routes that he thought were within my range. He also made sure that he did the leading. The agreement between us was unspoken but perfectly clear: it was my rat that was being fed, not his.

These days my rat is dormant and on the rare occasions when Mo climbs with me it is always on short, inconsequential routes, and for old times' sake. But secretly, I suppose, I still hankered to do one last serious climb with him, and maybe even have one last minor epic, before I hung up my boots. The chance came when a friend called me in the summer of 1985 to ask if I wanted to climb the Old Man of Hoy. The friend was George Band, who was a member of the first successful Everest expedition, in 1953, and, two years later, with Joe Brown, made the first ascent of Kanchenjunga. Since then, he has climbed equally effectively through the oil business and is now Director-General of UKOOA, the United Kingdom Offshore Operators Association, which provides the companies involved in British offshore oil with a channel through which to communicate with the outside world, and with a forum for internal discussion. In other words, he is a man for whom the oil companies like doing favours. So when Occidental Oil invited him to visit their oil terminal on Flotta, one of the Orkney Islands that lie off the north-east tip of Scotland, and he countered with the suggestion that while he was at it he might as well bring some friends along and climb the Old Man of Hoy, Oxy immediately agreed to organize the trip.

Band, who is my age – we were fifty-six at the time – invited his friend Richard Sykes, three years younger, and the twenty-year-old Peter Evans, whose father had been with Band on Everest in 1953. When Band called me, I suggested Mo, and Mo suggested the 33-year-old Paul Trower, one of the most talented climbers among the self-exiled Englishmen in Llanberis. Whatever else we managed, we would at least be the Old Man's oldest men: 264 years among the six of us, an average age of forty-four. Without Peter Evans, the average jumped to almost forty-nine. Oxy added two non-climbers to the party: a photographer called Chris Mikami and a young man from the public relations department, Alex Blake-Milton, to organize the logistics.

The Old Man is a sea stack, a rock tower rising straight out of the Atlantic on the north-west coast of the island of Hoy. I had seen it twice, in 1967 and 1984, but only on BBC television. Both times, it had looked like my ideal of climbing: a wild and beautiful place, steep rock, sunshine, the sea far below. But on first sight, from a distance, at about half past eight on a grey Saturday morning in September of 1985, it looked almost disappointing, certainly quite harmless.

An hour and a half earlier, when we had gathered on the dock at Stromness, the streets had gleamed with rain, the quayside had been patched with puddles. Then there had been a half-hour ride on a bucking ferry, past Graemsay lighthouse, still winking away in the morning air, across the mouth of Scapa Flow, towards the big dark hump of Hoy, which alone among the low-lying Orkneys has real hills and steep cliffs dropping off into the sea. Behind Hoy, the clouds in the western sky were black, but as we rolled and pitched across the bay a low sun came slanting in from the east, picking out the granite houses of Stromness behind us. On the island of Graemsay was an old stone fort and a line of derelict pill-boxes. In the middle of the channel – stern down, bow in the air – lay the mournful wreck of a merchant ship deliberately scuppered during the First World War to prevent German submarines from entering Scapa Flow, the huge natural harbour where the British fleet sheltered. Waves roared past it – the tide at this point flows at nine and a half knots – and its rusting bridge was lined with seabirds, mostly cormorants, like gloomy commuters waiting for the morning train. Other cormorants – long-necked, graceless birds – skimmed the surface of the water, searching for breakfast. We sat in the stern of the boat and watched the wind whip the white horses across the bay while

Chris Mikami moved busily about, taking his official photographs.

'For the obituaries,' said Mo.

The ferry deposited us at the little pier on Hoy and left in a hurry, as though the island were contaminated. By the pier was a small locked building, like an outhouse, and beside it, on a post, stood a sternly worded metal noticeboard:

OLD MAN OF HOY. CLIMBERS ARE HEREBY WARNED THAT THERE IS NEITHER SUITABLE RESCUE EQUIPMENT NOR EXPERIENCED ROCK CLIMBERS IN THE VICINITY. CLIMBERS THEREFORE PROCEED AT THEIR OWN RISK.

Parked at the pier was a mini-van, loaded with our equipment, that had been ferried over from Stromness the previous day. We drove across the island in silence, watching the rabbits scatter off the road into the heather. It was raining again. Then the sun slid out through a hard blue slit in the clouds and a great rainbow stood briefly between the hills that guard Rackwick, a scattered handful of stone cottages above a wide bay, with high yellowy-orange cliffs along its farther shore.

We parked the van by Rackwick Youth Hostel, loaded ourselves up with ropes and rucksacks, and plodded off on the long path that cuts upwards across the flank of the hills behind the village to the blunt crest of a ridge. Beyond the ridge was a wide curving moor –four parts heather to one part boggy peat–edged by cliffs that vanished into the sea. At its north-west corner, a mile or so away, beyond the farthest headland, the Old Man pointed into the air like a child's sketch of a factory chimney – a wobbly outline and slanted, grassy top. It seemed a paltry little thing, no more than fifty feet higher than the adjacent headland. I wondered what all the fuss was about and did not find out until I had slogged across the moor to the headland, gone to its edge and looked down.

A hundred yards away, at the end of a rocky promontory that was once a rock arch and is now a jumble of boulders, the Old Man sticks straight up out of the Atlantic, like the admonishing finger of God. The plinth it stands on is granite (that explains why it was not swept long ago into the sea), but the Old Man itself is Orcadian sandstone, the colour of terracotta, 450 feet high and square-cut, its top roughly the same area as its base. Its central section, however, swells out a little, like middle-age spread, and that means that on whichever face you climb at least one section will always overhang significantly. It looked like a ramshackle and overhanging version of London's Post Office Tower – 'disproportionate to the fragility of us', as David Jones wrote of the artillery barrages on the Western Front in the First World War. If I'd known I was going to climb *that*, I thought, I'd have done some training.

The sun had come out again, but a strong south-westerly was blowing in from the Atlantic, smashing the waves high up around the granite plinth, and far out to sea slanting grey columns of rain were moving steadily in our direction. Someone once said of sex, 'When it's good it's marvellous, and when it's bad it's still pretty good.' The Old Man of Hoy looked as if it were going to be something like that: when it's hard it's desperate, and when it's easy it's still pretty hard.

Our plan was to do the original and easiest route, up the East Face. This was first climbed in 1966 by a strong three-man team: Rusty Baillie, Tom Patey and Chris Bonington. But even they had climbed the crux—the long, overhanging second pitch–by artificial means: pitons, étriers, a tension traverse. Since then, the rules of the game have changed and the whole route, including the overhang, is now climbed free. The technical grade is 5a, Hard Very Severe. 'Just your style,' Mo had assured me, meaning that it was mostly a matter of brute strength, not technique. And perhaps it would have been my style ten years before, when I was in my middle forties and still relatively fit. Now I wasn't so sure. I had just returned from a month in Italy, where, on the strength of what Mo had told me, I had climbed for only a couple of days and had spent the rest of the time practising what Mo calls 'Egyptian P.T.'; that is, I had been lying on my back in the sun with my eyes closed.

Both Paul and Mo had climbed the Old Man before: Paul once, ten years earlier; Mo several times in his capacity as a climbing cameraman for the second BBC spectacular. So they knew what was involved–a long and hard climb, a difficult descent, and three old buffers who probably shouldn't be trying it–and had made their plans accordingly. Paul, who is an exceptionally strong climber, would lead the whole route. Mo would follow him, cleaning out all the gear Paul used except what might be needed by the rest of us. Then the three golden oldies would follow, in descending order of decrepitude: myself, George, Dick. Peter would come last, removing the rest of the protection that Mo had left in place. On the difficult second pitch, Paul would climb with a tail rope hanging free behind him which Mo would tie off at the first belay, so that when Paul abseiled down on the way back there would be a rope in place with which to pull himself across the traverse. The plan was for the lead climbers to be on their way back down, fixing the abseils, before Dick and Peter reached the summit. With six people roped together, speed was important, since by the time we had changed into climbing boots, sorted the gear and set off on the descent from the headland, it was already about eight-forty-five and the ferry was due to collect us from the far side of the island at five-thirty; that meant being back at the bottom of the Old Man no later than four.

We scrambled cautiously down the steep wet grass from the top of the headland to the little promontory that joins the Old Man to the rest of Hoy. From there, if you lie back on the boulders and look up, only the bottom half of the sea stack is visible, bulging out like a great, roughly thrown terracotta pot. The weather report had predicted sunshine, showers and hail, with south-westerly winds of twenty-five to thirty knots, gusting to forty knots. From down below, it felt as if they had underestimated the strength of the wind (they had), but the rest seemed accurate. The rain had come and gone as we trudged up from Rackwick, then come and gone again, but now a bright sun shone and the sea had changed from dirty grey to a strong deep blue. Out in the Atlantic, shafts of sunlight moved like searchlights across the water; farther out still were slanting columns of rain. But at least our route, up the landward East Face, would be out of the wind.

Paul checked the rack of gear at his waist, then put on a flimsy-looking safety helmet, white and ribbed, with a natty little brim.

'What's that?' I asked.

'A French piss pot. I only wear it to upset Mo.'

The first pitch goes up an eighty-foot pillar that leans against the Old Man's south-east corner. The climbing was steep and easy, although the curiously textured sandstone felt slippery and slightly unstable beneath the fingers, as though it had been dusted with hundreds-and-thousands, the coloured grains of sugar used in decorating children's cakes. The ledge at the top of the pillar, where Mo and Paul were waiting, was large and comfortable but exposed to the full force of the south-westerly. Immediately I was belayed, Paul set off on the hard pitch, while Mo paid out his rope and peered intermittently around the corner of the East Face to watch his progress. Meanwhile, I brought up George, he brought up Dick, and Dick eventually brought up Peter, so the ledge was as crowded as a rush-hour bus and festooned with gear and brightly coloured ropes. By that time, Mo was already halfway up the next pitch.

The only description of the route I had read was by Chris Bonington, who is a fine mountaineer but not famous for his accurate memory. This is what he wrote of the difficult section: 'An airy downward traverse leads into a small niche roofed by a square-cut overhang; an awkward hand-jam enables the climber to pull over this on to another small ledge, where he is once again in balance.'

'It's got one hard move,' Mo had told me over the telephone before I left home. Later, on the stance, he emended that to 'thirty difficult feet'. Paying out the rope, I watched him climb down for ten feet, then move cautiously across the traverse to a niche below an overhang, which he went over smoothly, hardly pausing. He shouted, 'There's a good layback hold on the edge round the corner!' Then he disappeared from sight.

The rope went out steadily again, then stopped for what seemed to be a long time. That part is not supposed to be too hard, I thought; he must be having trouble taking out Paul's gear. From far above, where Paul was belayed on the second stance, a loop of rope hung down over the overhang, several feet clear of the rock face. Occasionally, the wind gusted around the corner and blew it out until it was almost horizontal. The sun came and went. Whenever it shone, the long shadow of the Old Man lay dark on the water, pointing to a distant headland, and the breakers, thundering into the beach, flung rainbows back into the air.

The rope in my hands began to move again, though still very slowly. Another pause, then the slack rope between Mo and me was pulled in tight. Because of the wind and the roar of the breakers, there was no way to communicate with each other, but the photographer, Chris Mikami, who was lying on his back on the boulders below, lowered his camera for a moment and flapped his arms to indicate that it was time for me to move. Young Peter Evans, huddled against the wind in the farthest corner of the big ledge, fumbled in his anorak and pulled out a chicken leg wrapped in foil. He waved it triumphantly and shouted, 'Packed lunches! This is the life!'

I stepped off the comfortable ledge and moved round the corner out of the wind. Although the first pitch had been a mere eighty feet long, the promontory below the East Face dropped sharply away, and the exposure was suddenly considerable: 200 feet or more, straight down to the sea-washed boulders. I looked down once, then concentrated on the rock in front of my nose. Very carefully, I lowered myself ten feet to a line of small footholds that led across to the nichc. The footholds were widely spaced and there was only one obvious handhold, a little vertical slot at shoulder height. I slid the fingers of my right hand into it, pulled across, got my left hand, facing outwards, where my right hand had been, and stood tentatively in balance. I could see a foothold a long step across to the right but no hold for the right hand. Just above my head was a small, outward-sloping ledge, covered with hundreds-and-thousands, but when I tried to pull on it the fingers of my right hand immediately slid off. I brushed it, tried again, moved my left fingers next to my right, and stepped gingerly across. Jesus. Because no one had mentioned the traverse and Mo had sauntered across without bothering to take the cigarette out of his mouth, I assumed I was climbing badly. (Paul, who is as short as I am, later said he found the traverse as hard as anything on the climb.)

I found myself in a niche capped by an overhang – just what Bonington had described. On the right wall was a slot. When I reached up for it, my fingers sank most of the way in and its edge was good. I pulled, moved my feet up quickly on a couple of shadowy ledges, jammed my left hand in a crack above the overhang, found Mo's layback hold on the edge above, and was round the overhang, standing in balance at the foot of a steep corner with a crack at its back. If that's all there is to it, I thought, I'm home and dry.

Right in front of my nose, Mo's red-and-blue anorak and Paul's denim jacket were hanging from a piton in the crack. It seemed odd that they should have bothered to take them off *after* the crux. I looked up. A dozen feet above, the walls of the corner I was standing in closed inward and became a smooth, coffin-shaped, bottomless chimney capped by a rock roof that jutted out horizontally for about four feet. The rope from Mo to me came down through a crack on the left-hand side of this overhang, well clear of the rock face. Bonington's description was wrong: there were two overhung niches, not one, and it was the second that meant business.

I wormed my way up the corner until my helmet was scraping against the roof. Then I wriggled round so that I was facing outward, and jammed myself between the vertical walls to consider the situation. What was now the left-hand wall was blank except for a small indentation high up under the roof that might serve as a toehold. There were no holds at all on the other wall, but two slings dangled from the crack above it. One was threaded through an ancient wooden wedge that had probably been put there on the first ascent, nineteen years before; the other had been inserted by Paul. I rested again, staring out at the view. The young man from Occidental Oil was standing on the headland, leaning sharply forward into the wind. Down on the promontory, the photographer was still lying on a boulder and peering up through the viewfinder of his camera. Off to my left, the breakers crashed into the shore, creamy against the green water.

I wriggled round until I was facing the rock again. The proper way to climb the overhang was to jam my left fist into the crack from which the slings dangled and use it to pull around the lip. But when I tried that my hand could get no proper purchase and my fist slid out. I told myself that speed mattered more than style, and took hold of both slings and pulled, trying to get my right toe to stick on the shadowy indentation high on the wall. On the left of the overhang, at eye-level, was an outward-sloping foothold. The crack above, with the wooden wedge jammed in it, looked wide and reassuring. I heaved and swung my left foot up on to the high hold. But as I did so my right foot slipped off the little indentation. I lurched back down on the slings and jammed myself again across the corner. I simply could not see how I was going to make the move.

I knew what was needed: a big pull with the arms, a wide straddle with the feet, a dynamic upward movement, then a rest in balance. Just my style, as Mo had said, remembering the old days. I should have trained for this, I thought. It's a serious climb and I haven't taken it seriously. But in your middle fifties training isn't something you can take seriously, either. Then I realized that the rope coming down to me was as solid as the rock itself. With Mo above me, I wasn't going anywhere but up.

Before we started, I had taken the precaution of clipping into my waist harness a 'cow's tail', a loop of nylon cord with a fiffi-hook at one end. A fiffi-hook is about the size of a crooked finger, and when slipped into a piton or a sling it will take your weight and allow you to rest. It is a continental device for use on artificial aid routes, where you climb from piton to piton, and it is not approved of by British free-climbing purists. But where I was, jammed beneath a holdless four-foot overhang, climbing ethics were the least of my problems. I wormed my way up until my shoulders were pressed against the roof and I could slip the fiffi-hook into one of the slings that dangled in front of my nose. I rested again, hanging there like a sack of coal, until the feeling began to come back into my fingers. Then, with most of my weight supported by the sling, I plastered my right foot on the little indentation, grabbed the other sling and, pivoting on the cow's tail, heaved myself around the lip of the overhang, swung my other foot up on to the high left hold, and got my left hand comfortingly around the wooden wedge in the crack above. For the first time in what seemed hours – it was probably ten minutes – I was standing in balance again, leaning into the rock and panting like an old dog. When I looked down, all I could see was the water swaying around the base of the tower far below my feet. Above me, the crack went straight up, gently overhanging, for fifty feet. At its top, craning down at me, was Mo's grinning face. He waved.

'Watch the rope!' I shouted.

The crack was too wide for comfortable hand jams and the walls on either side of it bulged slightly outwards. But at least they were broken by occasional sloping ledges. My arms were pumped up by the struggle with the overhang, my shoulders ached, my fingers felt like ripe bananas. I had no alternative but to use my feet – and what little technique I could muster. I bridged tentatively up the corner, trying to do nothing that would strain my fingers, while Mo, to his everlasting credit, kept the rope as tight as a cello string.

When I finally wobbled on to the ledge where he and Paul were belayed, he looked at my drained face, grinned evilly, and said, 'I knew you'd love it.'

'You told me one move.'

'I told you thirty feet.'

'I psyched myself up for the wrong bit.'

'That's what comes of reading Bonington. At your age you should know better.'

Paul was already off again, moving up the rounded, muddy-looking rocks above. The rope went out quickly and the angle seemed easier, but that did not necessarily mean much. Paul is small and skinny, and looks like a rather intellectual pirate: a dark unshaven face below a high and narrow forehead; intelligent eyes; a gold ring in one ear. He and Mo once set some kind of record when they spent three days on the North Face of the Midi in midwinter, not because the conditions were bad but because they had started with dreadful hangovers and kept oversleeping on the bivouacs. Although Paul appears slight enough to be blown away by any wind, he climbs without noticeable effort–smoothly, precisely, unconcerned. It was like having a greyhound on a long lead, with Mo–more deliberate and more obviously powerful–as the keeper reining him in.

While Paul picked his way delicately up the next pitch, I pulled in the rope between myself and the next geriatric, George Band. Down on the promontory, the photographer waved his arms about to tell George his time had come, then applied himself again to his viewfinder. 'It's a long climb,' Mo had said. 'A long day. We've got to keep moving.' But lounging on the comfortable ledge, with the hardest part over and nothing to do except to keep the rope to George tight, I began finally to relax. The day darkened, a squall of rain hissed down. I pulled up the hood of my anorak and hunched over to light my pipe. By the time it was going, the shower had passed. The bay below was full of pale shapeless blobs of seaweed, like brain matter, that swayed backwards and forwards, merged into the foam of the breakers, then reappeared. The roar of the waves and the howling wind isolated each of us in his own world. When Mo, who was sitting next to me, asked for a light, he had to shout. When I looked round again, he was halfway up the next pitch, climbing towards Paul.

Climbers have a curiously Oriental attitude to their sport: except in extreme circumstances, they are less bothered about losing their lives than about losing face. They don't think of falling off in terms of broken limbs; falling off is a way of looking foolish to your peers, and a broken arm or leg is an outward and visible sign of inward and spiritual disgrace. Whenever climbers watch each other perform, *Schadenfreude* is high on their list of satisfactions. So although I should have been worrying about speed, I was secretly relieved when the rope between myself and George, who is my exact contemporary, came in inch by inch and with long pauses. I juggled with it occasionally, while I flexed my aching fingers, but only when I was sure I had it as taut as Mo had kept it for me. That, too, was part of an unspoken agreement. All three of us old men were climbing out of our class, so it was important to help one another out unobtrusively in order to keep our united face.

Before we started, Paul had said, 'At the top of the hard pitch, there's the best belay in the world:

a big thread with five million tapes round it.' Mo said, 'When we're done, there'll be five million and one.' The thread was, indeed, a miniature geological-mountaineering marvel: a little pillar four inches in diameter, bridging an open mouth of rock from upper lip to lower lip. Around it was a great mass of slings of all ages and colours: nylon-webbing tapes, old bits of full-weight rope, loops of Perlon cord of varying thicknesses. Some of them had been there so long that the weather had washed their colour away, leaving them grey and furry. Each party must have contributed at least one new sling for the abseil down. I began idly to count them but had reached only twenty when George's white helmet appeared at the edge of the overhang below and his strained face peered grimly up at me. He seemed dismayed at what he saw. His face disappeared, but one arm, like a snail's feeler, groped blindly for the wooden wedge in the crack. I leaned back on the rope to take his weight. Another pause, then the rope began to come in again, inch by inch by inch. When he finally pulled himself wearily on to the belay ledge he was grinning like a schoolboy. All he said was, 'Blimey!'

The next two pitches threaded their way quite easily through the muddy-textured but more gently angled rock that forms the Old Man's waist. The moment I reached Mo, at the third belay, Paul was off again to a stance at the foot of the steep final pitch. Mo had joined him there, and Paul had climbed to the summit and roped back down to Mo, while I still waited for Sykes to join Band at the top of the hard pitch. Although

Sykes was the fittest of us three oldies, he seemed to take longest negotiating the big overhang—perhaps because he is a stickler for climbing etiquette and was therefore reluctant to pull on the slings left in place. Neither George nor I had been so choosy, particularly since we knew that no one could see what went on under the overhang.

Another squall of rain came and went. I watched the photographer lug his heavy bag of gear painfully up the precipitous grass to the headland. When he reached the top he collapsed face down in the heather, where Alex Blake-Milton was patiently waiting.

The sun returned briefly, but had gone again by the time George joined me at the third stance. The air was darkening steadily as I climbed towards the foot of the last pitch. It was a clean-cut crack up a corner, plumb vertical, leading straight to the summit, and, like everything else on the Old Man of Hoy, it looked intimidating. But Mo climbed it as fast as if he were running upstairs, pausing only once, straddled across the corner, to shout down to me, 'You're gonna love this!' By then the sky had darkened still more and hail was lashing down like pellets from an air-gun. Over on the unprotected headland, the two spectators huddled miserably together, their backs to us and the storm.

The rope at my waist went tight. I glanced up, saw Mo wave at me, then ducked my head while the hail zinged off my helmet. Yet the pitch, after all, was beautiful: sharp handholds in the crack and, on either side of it, little ledges for the feet to bridge on.

About ten feet up, I was suddenly pushed outwards by the wind. In its top three-quarters, the crack goes clean through the whole tower, as if a giant had tried to split the Old Man with an axe. When I applied my eye to the crack, I could see right through to where thick veils of hail swayed over the Atlantic.

Mo was hunched on a ledge a few feet below the top. In his red helmet, red anorak and blue hood, he looked like a despondent garden gnome.

I said, 'What about the summit?'

'Been there before,' he answered. 'Be my guest.'

I scrambled up to the top and rested my backside briefly on the wiry grass. The wind howled around me, and when I tried to look out to sea I got a faceful of hail. By the time I was back on the ledge, Mo had already fixed the rope for the abseil down. 'We're getting a whole year's weather in one day,' I said. 'Everything but snow and fog.'

'It's not over yet.'

'Don't tell me – we're halfway there.'

'On this bugger, not even half.'

Mo attached himself to the abseil rope and swung briskly down. The moment he reached the stance below, Paul was off on the next abseil, as though he and Mo were running a relay race.

In the meantime, George had grunted his way carefully up the final crack. He looked at his watch when he arrived and announced, 'Four minutes to four.'

'No wonder they're in a hurry.'

The hail had eased a little but the wind did not let up.

'Not a lot of laughs on top,' I said.

'Must be done,' George answered. 'For posterity's sake.'

He heaved himself up the last few feet to the summit and staggered around for a minute or two while the gale tried to blow him off. Across on the headland the photographer was still huddled miserably against the wind with his back to us. So much for posterity. But when George climbed back down on to the ledge he wore a smile I could have warmed my hands on. 'I never thought we'd do it,' he said.

Although abseiling looks like the most spectacular of all mountaineering procedures, it is in fact the simplest. The climber clips a doubled rope into a belay sling, threads it through a braking device, called a descendeur, that is attached to his waist harness – in Britain the device is usually an alloy figure-of-eight – then slides down the rope, using his left hand to steady himself on the rope above and, with his right, paying out the rope from below through the descendeur. As he slides down, he pushes himself away from the rock with his feet. To the outsider, it looks like a spider letting itself down on its own thread, a daring and improbable feat. In practice, even a beginner can pick up the knack in minutes, once he has swallowed his fear of launching himself out into space and has learned to trust his gear.

The first three abseils from the summit of the Old Man were simple. The only problem was the big, hard pitch. Not only did it overhang considerably – so that on the way back down we would be dangling well clear

of the rock – it also involved a traverse: as we faced the
rock, the stance we were aiming for was twenty feet or
more off to the left. Paul had solved that problem by
climbing the pitch with a spare rope trailing free behind
him. He had attached it to the second belay and Mo had
made the bottom end fast below, leaving a fixed rope
running diagonally across the pitch between the first
and second stances. On the descent, Paul would use
this rope to guide himself down and pull across to the
lower belay. Mo would release the fixed rope before he
followed, and Paul would simply pull him and the rest
of us across with the free end of the abseil rope.

Mo was preparing to leave the stance above the hard
pitch when I arrived. Our new sling had been added to
the dozens already in place around the giant thread, and
Mo leaned out against it, double-checking for safety.

'Whatever you do, try not to bounce around too
much,' he said.

Then he disappeared down the climb. A couple of
minutes later, I felt the abseil rope go slack: he had
arrived at the stance below.

I clipped into the rope and began to slide down,
my feet only just in contact with the walls of the
steep corner above the overhang. I noticed that I was
not quite as upright as I should have been, and paused
for a moment on the lip of the overhang to try to get
a better balance. Then I stepped off into space and slid
on down, hanging free. But as I did so my feet tipped
up until I was almost horizontal, and I began to gyrate
slowly so that I was facing away from the rock, with my

boots pointing towards the land. I tried to pull myself up with my left hand, but to do that I needed to ease some of the downward part of the rope through the descendeur; and the downward rope was held tight by Paul, who was trying to pull me across to the stance. I went on turning in the breeze, like a rotisserie chicken, while my feet began to tilt – very slowly, very gently – above my head.

'Try not to bounce around too much,' Mo had said. But he hadn't mentioned anything about turning upside down. For one long minute, I thought I was going to slide head first out of my harness.

'Perfect love casteth out fear,' they say. And perfect fear casteth out exhaustion. I pulled with all the strength that remained in my left arm until my head was just above the axis of my feet. Out of the corner of my eye, I saw Paul, on the stance, staring at me in astonishment. He shouted over his shoulder to Mo, 'Come and talk to Al! He's gone horizontal!'

From the comfort of the big ledge, Mo's voice wafted back: 'Any excuse to put his feet up!'

Together they heaved on the rope and manhandled me, feet first, round the corner and on to the ledge.

I lay on my back, puffing like a walrus and knowing, finally, that I was too old for long, serious climbs. My left hand was so numb from my one-arm pull-up that I could scarcely hold my pipe to light it.

Mo looked at me solemnly. 'The youth hostels run courses on abseiling,' he said. 'If you pass, they give you a nice badge.'

When I at last managed to stagger to my feet, I saw what had gone wrong. At the start of the climb, I had fastened my waist harness over my anorak and North Cape jacket, to keep myself warm during the long wait on the windy first stance. As I climbed, I had unzipped my anorak and jacket and pulled them free but I had forgotten to tighten the belt of the harness. During the abseil, the harness had slipped from my waist to my upper thighs, shifting my centre of gravity.

I said, 'There always has to be one clown in every party. But why does it have to be me?'

Mo said, 'What worried me was going back to your wife with your knickers and pink socks and saying, "Al's gone." '

I pulled up my harness and tightened it, then roped down the easy first pitch, while the other two waited on the stance to help George over the difficult abseil. On the promontory, I paused to look back up the climb. Up and up and up. My neck creaked with the effort. I was too weary even to feel pleased at having got up the brute. Peter Evans and Dick Sykes were still sorting out ropes at the foot of the top pitch. It would be a long time yet. I had not brought a watch with me, and the sun had long vanished behind cloud, but the day felt greyer and later than it should have if we were to meet the ferry at half past five. I picked up a rucksack full of spare gear and began to slog back up the steep, slippery grass to the headland. When I thought I was out of sight of those still on the Old Man, I stopped to rest, and went on stopping every few steps all the way to the top. Unfortunately, Mo spotted me as I crept upwards. 'Your speed was barely discernible,' he said later. 'It was like watching a sun dial.'

Chris Mikami and Alex Blake-Milton were waiting on the headland, cold and wet and irritable. The first thing I said was, 'What's the time?' It was five-fifteen and we were still an hour away from the pier. The captain of the ferry had agreed to come back at six-thirty if we didn't show on time, but the others were not yet off the climb. (I could see Peter roping down the third pitch while Dick got ready to abseil over the big overhang.) There is no hotel on Hoy, or even a pub, and we hadn't brought sleeping bags. The best we could hope for was a cold hungry night in the youth hostel barn.

'We'd better get motoring,' I said.

'What about my group shot with the Old Man in the background?' the photographer asked.

'What about a beer and a meal and a comfortable bed?'

They set off unwillingly while I sat with my back to the gale and ate some of my packed lunch. Then I trudged after them across the bog.

It seemed a long way. The rain had made the track even muddier than before and I kept coming down on my backside in the ooze. Even the downhill stretch to the stone cottages at Rackwick felt endless. Another squall of rain came and went. Then the evening sun appeared and, with it, a vivid, perfect rainbow with one foot on the eastern hills, the other on the beach at Rackwick Bay.

The van was waiting with its engine running and its heater on. Even before I asked, Blake-Milton said, 'It's six-thirty now, but don't worry. I called the coastguard and the ferry is picking us up at half past seven.'

I sat on the back step of the van and chewed my way through what was left of my packed lunch. The others –fitter than I was and just as anxious not to miss the boat–arrived within twenty minutes. We were across the island and at the pier with half an hour to spare. Then we sat with music blaring from the van's tape machine while the evening light faded and the windows misted up.

Mo lit a fresh cigarette from the stub of his old one and said contentedly, 'It's like a workmen's bus in here.'

At seven-twenty-five, we emptied the van, locked it, and lugged our gear on to the pier. The last light had almost gone, the wind had risen and it had begun to rain again. The beam from the lighthouse on Graemsay flashed across the bay; beyond it, a few lights glimmered on the main island, west of Stromness. There was no sign of the boat. We stamped up and down the pier and stared out into the rain from under the hoods of our anoraks. Blake-Milton peered at his watch every few seconds and muttered grimly to himself. No one else spoke. Then, suddenly, the ferry was quite close, a dark shape on the dark water, a red light and a green light moving briskly towards us. Within two minutes of its touching the pier, we were on board with all our gear and the boat was off again, bucking and rolling as the rain built swiftly into another squall. On Flotta, at the far end of Scapa Flow, Occidental's North Sea oil terminal, which is so sculpted into the landscape as to be almost invisible by day, was lit up like a city. In the ferry's cabin, below decks, the three oldies slumped on benches, too exhausted to speak, while Mo and Paul did one-arm pull-ups on the roof beams in celebration.

As we sidled up to the jetty in Stromness, Mo said, 'How's your rat, then?'

'He overate,' I answered. 'I think he just died.'

11
Everest

There were sixteen climbers in the 1986 British North-East Ridge of Everest Expedition – a name, Mo remarked, that 'fair trips off the tongue'. The leader was 'Brummie' Stokes who had been to the top of Everest in 1976 and had lost all his toes from frostbite on the way down. Stokes had been a sergeant-major in the Special Air Services, and ten of his 1986 Everest team had also served in the Army, either in the SAS or the Royal Marines. The five civilians were Mo, Joe Brown, Bill Barker, Clive Rowlands and Paul Nunn. All fifteen were selected on the principle that Mo has always applied to his own trips: 'Their faces had to fit before they were even asked.' Between them, they had a great deal of big mountain experience and also – for Everest – an unusual number of years spent in acquiring it. Joe celebrated his fifty-sixth birthday on the mountain and Mo had his forty-seventh in Peking, on the way in. 'A dismal affair,' he said. 'I sat there with a bottle of beer singing "Happy birthday to me". Everyone else had gone to bed.'

The expedition left England on 31 July, 1986, and reached Everest, via Peking and Lhasa, on 8 August. By that time, however, they had already had one of their best moments, and it took place in Liverpool, not on Everest. About six months before they set out, they met up at the family home of Paul Moores, the deputy leader, to pack the gear that had to be freighted in advance to China. In the evening, when the packing was done, they went off for a beer at the local, then drifted idly back to the house in twos and threes, an ex-Marine called Sam Roberts in front, Mo and Bill Barker just behind him. When Roberts opened the front door a shadowy figure burst past him. Roberts yelled, 'Stop him! He's a burglar.' Mo, who had been a keen rugger player before he discovered climbing, made a flying tackle, knocked the man to the ground and pinned his arms behind his back. As the rest of the expedition strolled out of the fog – twelve massive figures, most of them trained in unarmed combat – Mo murmured in the man's ear, 'This is not your lucky night.' The burglar, who subsequently served thirteen months for breaking and entering, was relieved when the police came to arrest him.

By modern standards, a sixteen-man team is very large and has drawbacks Mo had never encountered before. 'It can become kind of impersonal. You find you're working for long periods of time without seeing three-quarters of the expedition. At the beginning, for example, Joe, Bill Barker, Paddy Freeny and myself went out to establish Advanced Base Camp and we were away two weeks without seeing anyone. In fact, it was very enjoyable, because we were going where no one had ever been before, and everything was new. But after we'd got Advanced Base in and were near where Camp

1 would be, it was time to go down for a rest. On the way back to Base Camp we passed Paul Moores and Sam Roberts coming uphill. We spent an evening with them in the crossing camp, and that was it. Then they were on the hill putting in Camps 1 and 2, and by the time we got back up to Advanced Base they were on their way down again. And so it goes. But these are mates it would be nice to spend time with, and the only chance you get is when there is a long spell of bad weather and everybody goes down to Base Camp. That's when you think, oh yes, *he's* on this trip, isn't he? For me, an expedition loses something when that happens.'

The second drawback was a result of the Chinese refusal to provide porters. Mo again: 'To place one bottle of oxygen in the top camp, about twenty loads have to leave Base Camp. You need fixed ropes for the steep bits, tents for the intermediate camps, food and fuel to stock them, more oxygen cylinders to get up to the top camp, and so on. To put one person on the summit requires a very broad-based triangle of support. Then, when you've worked out the number of loads each member of the team is going to have to carry, you find that, say, fifty per cent of the people are unfit for carrying, so your load goes up and up. It's a mammoth task. I laughed like a drain when I read that the Chinese had used three or four hundred porters on their first ascent in 1960, but now I see why. Humping all those loads is not only tedious in the extreme, it also wears you out for no increase in height. Apart from depriving the

Sherpas of a job, all you're doing is exhausting yourself. And that can mean the failure of the expedition, because if you all get knackered carrying loads you're going to end up with no one who is fit enough to bat out the trail and go for the summit.'

As it turned out, the 1986 North-East Ridge Expedition failed to reach the summit of Everest, but not because of the lack of porters. Camp Two had been established at around 24,000 feet, and the lead climbers had reached a point about 1,500 feet higher when bad weather set in. 'Snow and very high winds,' said Mo. 'Not just blasts of wind but a steady gale, blowing non-stop.' They waited a week at Advanced Base for the storm to blow itself out, then went back down to Base Camp and waited another fortnight. But the wind still did not drop. Finally, after kicking their heels for three weeks, they went back up the mountain and two climbers, Trevor Pilling and Harry Taylor, used a faint lull in the weather to struggle to the foot of the notorious pillars. Then the wind got up again and they had to retreat. Mo's last view of Everest was from a lorry, driving back to Lhasa: 'I looked back and saw what seemed to be smoke coming out of a chimney on the summit. It was a five-mile tail of powder snow being blown off the top. When we arrived in August I thought we'd be able to see all the rock bands on the north side. Instead, Everest was like a Christmas cake, completely white. When we left, in October, it was black again. You'd think the cladding would come in winter, but the opposite is true. Most of the snow falls during the monsoon and gets blown away in winter.'

What had happened was quite simple. In 1986, the Himalayan winter came in a month early, and in winter the jet stream, that blows continually in the upper atmosphere, drops from about 30,000 feet to about 26,000. 'The jet stream dictates when and where you can climb,' said Mo. 'You can be in a howling gale on Everest while somebody else is having quite reasonable weather on a nearby peak a bit lower. Climbing Everest in winter, when the jet stream has dropped, is a very different ballgame from climbing it pre- or post-monsoon. The weather is far, far harsher, so your gear needs to be that much warmer – boots, gloves, down suits, tents, everything. It suddenly becomes much harder to survive than it is in normal Everest conditions. Those aren't exactly jolly, but they're an absolute doddle compared with what you get when it's really cold. I mean, the simple physical act of standing up in those winds is desperate. If you want to climb Everest in winter, you have to wait for a weather-window, when the jet stream lifts for a bit. We waited twenty-odd days and the window never opened.' That season, all the 8,000-metre peaks were affected by the premature arrival of winter. On K2, thirteen climbers died.

Nobody died on the North-East Ridge of Everest, but nobody seems to have had a lot of laughs, either, despite the care with which the team was chosen. Indeed, the whole expedition seemed so different from Mo's usual style that it was not altogether clear why he'd gone. 'I went because it was Everest,' he said. 'If the peak had been a couple of hundred feet lower, I'd have steered clear of a big expedition like that, no matter how much I liked the blokes who were going. But I'd always thought it would be nice to stand on the highest point in the world. I don't believe there is any climber who wouldn't want to do that. The question is whether or not standing there justifies the effort. There is no way I'm going to be asked on one of those modern-style trips where half a dozen young hotshots do it oxygen-free. I'm too old for that, not fit enough, not good enough. So when Brummie invited me I thought, I won't have many more opportunities to go for the top and in a couple of years I may not even want to. I ought to get it done now, while I can. And of all the routes on Everest, the North-East Ridge was the one that appealed most because it's unclimbed and it looked as if it would be fairly hard. If it had just been the South Col trade route, I don't think I'd have been interested.

'I had a preconceived idea that Everest was a boring mountain, and my first sight of it didn't make me change my mind. We drove over a pass, and there in the distance was this row of peaks with one marginally higher than the others. Everybody pulled out their cameras and started clicking away. But it didn't give me any buzz at all. Once you're on the hill, however, all that changes. Everest has a special atmosphere, an atmosphere like that of no other mountain, and gradually it gets to you. It's just so bloody big you feel you have to climb it. You see these huge expanses of rock and ice and

you think, that one small flank is bigger than any of the
mountains I've ever been on. It's difficult even to begin
to comprehend the size until you draw back and work
out what is where. For example, you're in Base Camp
at seventeen thousand and you look up at the North
Col, which is around twenty-three thousand, and realize
that there's another six thousand feet beyond that to the
summit. But because there's a lot of foreshortening on a
mountain the distance between the col and the summit
looks about a fifth of the distance between you and the
col, and it just doesn't seem possible that the two could
be the same. The scale is simply too large to take in.
It's a massive presence, the biggest thing in the world.
I think that is why it fascinates people and makes them
go back again and again. But I didn't find it a tense
type of hill. Gasherbrum, for instance, was dangerous
and gripping, and I expended an immense amount of
nervous energy on it. Everest was far more relaxed.
It's the height that gets you, and the size. You're
gasping away at twenty-four thousand feet and then
you think, I've still got five thousand more to go! On
the North-East Ridge route, everyone talks about the
pinnacles: once you're up them, you've cracked it, they
say. Not true. You're still seventeen hundred vertical
feet and three-quarters of a mile in distance from the
summit, and that's a long, long way when you're above
twenty-eight thousand. I mean, there are only a couple
of other places in the world that high. So it's by no
means over when you've done the pinnacles. You've
still got a full day to go.'

Apart from the scale of the mountain, I asked, had the climbing been interesting?

'Bits of it were OK,' Mo said. 'But in general you're so knackered that the interesting parts are only interesting in retrospect. At the time, they're a pain in the arse, because suddenly you've got to have your wits about you; you can't just go into overdrive and stamp up; you've got to start thinking; and thinking up there isn't easy. It's only afterwards, when you come down and look back up to where you've been, that you think, that was a good pitch. At that altitude, when you're faced with a technical challenge, all you want to do is get it out of the way. The easier the climbing is, the easier your path to the summit will be. In a way, you're arguing against yourself. You pick a route because it is interesting and difficult, but when you get to the interesting bits the altitude makes you wish they weren't there. This doesn't happen on lower peaks where you actually enjoy the climbing. But altitude slows you down, both physically and mentally. The only time it's pleasant is when you stop. You know this, of course, but you also know that the only way you're going to get up the thing is by moving. So it's a constant battle with yourself.

'You say to yourself, I'll do another hundred paces. Then you say, no, I'll do two hundred. I've always been a great counter. When I first climbed in the Alps I realized that if I had a rest whenever I felt sorry for myself I'd have too many rests. So I set myself targets. I'd say, right, I'll do five hundred paces. And I'd work out a position on the mountain where I thought five hundred paces would get me. I was always wrong. I'd do my five hundred and find I was about halfway. So I'd think, right, I won't rest after five hundred, I'll rest when I get there. So I'd do a thousand paces. Then I'd think, now I'll go a thousand paces between rests. Naturally, I'd cheat. If a step collapsed on me I'd think, shall I count that as one or shall I miss it out? No, I can't do that because all the odd numbers are on the left foot and that would blow the system. All these stupid things would be going through my head as I trudged upwards. On Everest, I was counting on a really grand scale. I knew the number of steps from Advanced Base across the glacier; I knew the number of steps up the first fixed rope, and the second, and the third. I always knew exactly where I was. I knew how many steps I'd done and how many I still had to do. I used to do mental arithmetic. I'd work out what fraction of the day I'd done, then I'd turn it into a percentage. I'd say to myself, if I do fifty steps, that's nought point six of a per cent of the morning's work. So I'd do the fifty and I'd think, that's ninety-nine point four per cent left to do. I was constantly having to revise my calculations. If it snowed and I had to put a new trail in, then the steps would be smaller and there would be more of them. That was a real pig, because in my mind the route had become longer! Counting is one way of cutting down on the boredom; it keeps you interested and helps get rid of the day. But I don't think any of the others did it. Bill Barker said he just thought about women.

'When I'm not counting, I time myself, like on that walk back from the Ogre. Both are ways of finding out if I am performing properly. And that's very important when you're at altitude. Making a cup of tea at twenty-five thousand feet can be a two-hour job: you have to get out of your warm sleeping bag in the dark, in horrible conditions, chip off ice and put it into the pot with your bare hands. It's all so much effort that you say, "Sod it, I won't bother." And it's easy to say "Sod it" to all the hundred and one little jobs you have to do on a trip – basic things, like keeping your sleeping bag dry. But if you don't do them you start to go downhill both physically and mentally. The mere size of a Himalayan peak is demoralizing. If you look up to the top and see that you've still got five or six or seven thousand feet to go, it can overpower you. You just have to get used to looking at the next rope-length and make sure you climb that properly. For me, counting and timing myself help me concentrate on what is in front of my nose. They are ways of keeping up my morale.'

I asked how long he thought he would keep going on expeditions. He answered, 'I can see a time might come when I'll say, "I've had enough of this, I can't hack it any more." But not yet. There are still all sorts of things I want to do and they don't necessarily involve hard routes on big peaks. The filming-climbing business interests me a lot. It would also be nice to wander around the Himalayas, going places where nobody's been and weighing up the star routes that are left; then you could go along to the young lads and say, "Here's a list that'll save you a lot of work." And there are even eight-thousand-metre mountains, like Broad Peak, that I'm sure I'll be able to walk up when I'm sixty. Outside the big ranges, there are plenty of places I want to go: Foula in the Shetlands, where I went ten years ago, and the Faroes, and the South American jungle again, and the islands in the Pacific—I bet they have acres of rock that no one has ever touched. Then there are things that have nothing to do with climbing. I'd like to go back to Alaska and have a go at one of the dog-sledge races, like the Iditerod. There's also a round-the-world single-handed driving record that I think would be easy to break. All sorts of things. After all, there are different grades of fitness. If you want to climb an eight-thousander in modern Alpine style, then you have to be very fit, mentally and physically. But if you want to go for a geriatric walk up Broad Peak, then the degree of fitness is far less. All I'm saying is that as you get older you tail off your objectives. There are some people who say, "If I can't climb the hardest routes, then I'm not going to climb anything." Well, fifteen years ago I used to climb semi-hard, but now my standard has dropped and it doesn't bother me at all. Eventually, I suppose, all I'll be capable of is pootly old walks, but I don't think there'll be any definite cut-off point. I can't see that happening, because I don't know what else I'd do except become incredibly bored.

'The truth is, I like an unforgiving climate where if you make mistakes you suffer for it. That's what turns me on. It's like the difference between windsurfing on Lake Como in the summer and off the coast of Maine in winter. One is a challenge, the other is a soft option, something you do at weekends when you want to have a good time. But every year you need to flush out your system and do a bit of suffering. It does you a power of good. I think it's because there is always a question mark about how you would perform. You have an idea of yourself and it can be quite a shock when you don't come up to your own expectations. If you just tootle along you can think you're a pretty slick bloke until things go wrong and you find you're nothing like what you imagined yourself to be. But if you deliberately put yourself in difficult situations, then you get a pretty good idea of how you are going. That's why I like feeding the rat. It's a sort of annual check-up on myself. The rat is you, really. It's the other you, and it's being fed by the you that you think you are. And they are often very different people. But when they come close to each other, that's smashing, that is. Then the rat's had a good meal and you come away feeling terrific. It's a fairly rare thing, but you have to keep feeding the brute, just for your own peace of mind. And even if you did blow it, at least there wouldn't be that great unknown. But to snuff it without knowing who you are and what you are capable of, I can't think of anything sadder than that.'

EPILOGUE

A few months after the Everest expedition, the Anthoines went skiing in the Alps over Christmas with two friends, Dave and Lynn Potts. On Christmas Day, Mo blacked out on a ski-lift and only Lynn's presence of mind and fast reactions prevented him from falling and breaking his neck. When the doctors examined him they found he had a tumour on the brain and rushed him to a hospital back in England.

I didn't find out about this until a couple of weeks later when I was going through the proofs of this book with an editor of the British edition and called Mo with a question about one of the illustrations. His mother-in-law answered the phone and told me what had happened. It seemed unthinkable that Mo the indestructible, who had survived fourteen expeditions to the Himalayas and Karakorum, where the fatality rate is one in seven, could have been ambushed by cancer.

A week later, I called him again. This time Jackie answered. They had operated the previous Thursday, she told me, and, according to the doctors, the signs were good. She thought so, too: by Monday Mo was already up and about in the hospital, doing press-ups and squats, and flirting with the nurses. He had also done the *The*

Times' notoriously tricky crossword puzzle in forty-seven minutes. 'I told him it must have been an easy one,' she said.

Three days later, I had another question about the captions, so I called again, this time from the publisher's office. Again, Jackie answered. 'Ask Mo,' she said. 'He's right here.' Mo's cheerful voice came on the line: 'Village idiot speaking.' I burst out laughing, mostly with relief. 'Laugh like that,' he said sternly, 'and I'll come down to London and give you a piece of my mind.' Then he added, 'I've got hundreds more like that.'

'Tell me what the doctors said.'

'The usual stuff. I asked the surgeon what he did with the hole he left in my head: pack it with Polyfilla? He answered "No, it just fills up naturally with what you would term slops".'

He was sorry but he couldn't stop to chat; they were off in forty-five minutes, back to the Alps, so Jackie could do some skiing. 'I'm going to sunbathe,' he said, without much conviction. In fact, within two days he was skiing black runs with her. This was ten days after four hours of major surgery. Three months later he was back on the North East Ridge of Everest with Brummie Stokes and the lads. I asked a mutual friend, Ian McNaught-Davis, how he thought brain surgery and high altitude would get along together. Mac shrugged: 'Better to die on a mountain doing something he loves than rot in hospital bed.'

The conditions on Everest in 1988 were worse than in '87, so Mo never made it to the summit. Before the year was out, the brain tumour had reappeared and he was on the operating-table again, thirteen months after the first operation. The hospital, ironically named Hope, was outside Manchester, in Eccles, where the cakes come from. Mac had been there the day before I went and had found the place apparently deserted – no one on the front desk, no one in the corridors, all the doors shut tight. Finally, a man in a white coat came bustling past. Mac, who is big and funny and impossible to ignore, blocked his way. 'Are all the patients cured then?' he barked. Mo was still cackling about that when I arrived, and he kept the jokes coming as usual. But he looked battered. His lips had retracted, his mouth and jaw-line were tight, his right eye was half-shut, the area around it was bruised and swollen, and there was a large surgical dressing on the side of his head. He looked like a man who had been mauled in a fight and was readying himself for the next round.

Not that he mentioned it. Although his prognosis was grim and he was about to start a course of chemotherapy, he talked in a matter-of-fact way about getting back on the rocks and about a filming job in Norway the following month: 'Nothing to it. They'll chopper me in and out. All I'll have to do is hold the camera.'

He was whistling in the dark of course, and he knew it, but he was also feeding the rat. 'Every year you need to flush out your system and do a bit of suffering,' he had said, 'because there's always a question of how you would perform.' Hence his bloody-minded determination not to go under, to feed the brute and fight it all the way. Mo had always had a genius for cracking jokes at his own expense. Once, when he was making a romantic pass at a girl, he whispered in her ear, 'This won't take long, did it?' The fooling around was his stylish way of coping with the Hobbesian truths he had learned at his stepmother's knee: if life is nasty, brutish and short, and extreme discomfort is the natural condition, then the best you can do is enjoy what's on offer for what it is, and have fun while you are about it. It was a style that had worked for him in the mountains; now it would have to work for him in this shabby hospital. He had taken a beating, his body was gaunt and his face was clenched, but there was nothing beaten about him. It was impossible to imagine he might die. Neither his will nor his sense of the ridiculous would allow it.

Two other climbers arrived while I was there, both of them almost bald, like me. Mo studied us beadily. 'You couldn't get a paintbrush out of the three of you,' he said.

All this time, Jackie was sitting silently at the end of his bed, stroking his foot.

The last time I saw Mo was four months later in June 1989. It was hot and sunny, a perfect day for climbing, though the weather was on the turn. Snowdon was bathed in light when I drove up the pass towards Llanberis, but there were storm-clouds massing behind it. I arrived at Tyn-y-Ffynnon as the district nurse was leaving. Mo was upstairs, propped up in a bed, wearing an Everest '88 t-shirt, and watching a Test match on television. He made jokes about the drugs he was taking and the chronic constipation they caused and the blessed enema the nurse had just administered. Then he muttered something about going back to the Himalayas next month and the big party he was planing for his fiftieth birthday in August – but vaguely, tuning in and out as the morphine took him.

Feeding The Rat had been published by then but he did not mention it. I think he was embarrassed to be the subject of a book and had only gone along with the idea because I was his friend and writing was how I made a living. The idea of being a hero, in however oblique a way, was not his style. It clashed with his pleasure principle: he went climbing to have fun with his pals and to go places where other people hadn't been; fame was not part of the equation. I think he was also bothered by how the notoriously back-biting climbing world would react. And he was bothered even more by what his mates would think of it.

Instead, he talked about Joe Simpson's recently published epic *Touching The Void*. When I said I hadn't read it, he swung his legs abruptly out of bed and made his way down the staircase – unsteadily, as though he found the going hard. Once he got to the bottom the drug kicked in again and he seemed to forget why he was there. He rummaged though the kitchen, the dining room, the back bedroom that used to be his and Jackie's, trying to remember what he was looking for. Finally, he found Simpson's book in the living room, handed it to me, then sat down heavily, unable to go any further.

'How's that stupid old dog of yours?' he asked.

'Gone. Paralysed. He had to be put down.'

'I know how he felt.'

His big, square head nodded and he drifted off for a moment. Then he swallowed some pills and laboured slowly back up the stairs to bed without saying a word. I gave him time to settle, then went up to say goodbye. He grinned faintly but was too exhausted to speak.

Mo died on 11th August, 1989, a few days after his fiftieth birthday, and was buried a week later. (I was stuck in Italy with guests, which I bitterly regret, so my children, Luke and Kate, who loved him, went in my place.) Four hundred people turned up for the funeral, so many that they overflowed the little chapel at Nant Peris and filled the cemetery outside. Jackie had wanted to read Miroslav Holub's poem, 'Love', but she wasn't up to it, so her father read it for her:

> Two thousand cigarettes.
>
> A hundred miles
>
> from wall to wall.
>
> An eternity and a half of vigils
>
> blanker than snow.
>
> Tons of words
>
> old as the tracks

of a platypus in the sand.

A hundred books we didn't write.
A hundred pyramids we didn't build.

Sweepings.
Dust.

Bitter

as the beginning of the world.

Believe me when I say

it was beautiful.

Climbers, especially British climbers, are wary of show-
ing emotion, but by the end of the poem there wasn't a
dry eye or a stiff upper lip among them.

As Mo's coffin was lowered into the grave, a solitary
figure appeared high up on the ridge of Glynders, over-
looking Llanberis Pass. 'I reckon it was Mo,' Mac said,
'come back to have a last laugh at all the fuss.'

Al Alvarez, 2001

THE BIGGEST GAME IN TOWN   Al Alvarez
£7.99   0 7475 6299 7

Since its first publication twenty years ago, *The Biggest Game in Town* has become a cult classic. Al Alvarez delves into the murky and compelling world of high-stakes Vegas poker, where 'the next best thing to playing and winning is playing and losing'. Deftly capturing the skewed physics and peculiar rites of the professional poker players who descend on Vegas every year for the World Series of Poker, an exotic world is uncovered, a world that seems too eccentric, too amazing, and too extravagant to be true.

'Probably the best book on poker ever written' *Evening Standard*

'A marvellous book ... picturesque, funny and dramatic' *Sunday Telegraph*

'The ruthless, mind-boggling world of the poker professionals is vividly described ... an engrossing, shimmeringly well-written account of the world poker knockout championship' *Sunday Express*

'A new classic on gambling ... it's quite brilliant' *Time Out*

'A cool, precise, sharply witty, vivid evocation of a place and people, their appearances, behaviour and speech. Mr Alvarez is a shrewd analyst of the psychology of gamblers and a cleverly selective recorder of the bizarre talk with which, directly and indirectly, they reveal their secure grasp of unreality and their insane courage' *Sunday Telegraph*

To order from Bookpost PO Box 29 Douglas Isle of Man IM99 1BQ www.bookpost.co.uk
email: bookshop@enterprise.net fax: 01624 837033 tel: 01624 836000

bloomsburypbks

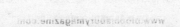

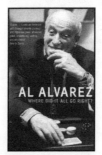